David Lathrop

The History of the Fifty-Ninth Regiment Illinois Volunteers

David Lathrop

The History of the Fifty-Ninth Regiment Illinois Volunteers

ISBN/EAN: 9783744740593

Printed in Europe, USA, Canada, Australia, Japan

Cover: Foto ©ninafisch / pixelio.de

More available books at **www.hansebooks.com**

COL. P. SIDNEY POST.

LIEUT. COL. C. H. FREDRICK.

LIEUT. COL. CLAYTON HALL.

MAJ. J. M. STOOKEY.

Dʀ H. J. MAYNARD.

ADJT. FRANK CLARK.

CAPT. MINNETT.

CAPT. J. C. HENDERSON.

THE HISTORY

OF THE

FIFTY-NINTH REGIMENT

ILLINOIS VOLUNTEERS,

OR A THREE YEARS' CAMPAIGN THROUGH MISSOURI, ARKANSAS, MISSISSIPPI, TENNESSEE AND KENTUCKY, WITH A DESCRIPTION OF THE COUNTRY, TOWNS, SKIRMISHES AND BATTLES—INCIDENTS, CASUALTIES AND ANECDOTES MET WITH ON THE WAY; AND EMBELLISHED WITH TWENTY-FOUR LITHOGRAPHED PORTRAITS OF THE OFFICERS OF THE REGIMENT.

BY DR. D. LATHROP.

HALL & HUTCHINSON,
PRINTERS AND BINDERS, INDIANAPOLIS, IND.
1865.

Entered according to Act of Congress, in the year one thousand eight hundred and sixty-five,

BY DR. DAVID LATHROP,

In the Clerk's Office of the District Court of the United States, for the District of Indiana.

HALL & HUTCHINSON, STEREOTYPERS, PRINTERS AND BINDERS.

INTRODUCTION.

Early in the month of May, 1861, C. H. Frederick and David McGibbon, two prominent citizens of St. Louis, Mo., called on General Lyon, and proffered to raise a regiment of infantry, to serve for three years, or during the war. C. H. Frederick, having previously served his country in a military capacity, and being familiar with military tactics, was deemed by General Lyon, a very suitable person to engage in the undertaking, and immediately authorized to recruit and organize a regiment, and to have command of the same.

Colonel Frederick, at the breaking out of the rebellion, was engaged in a lucrative business in St. Louis, but at the call of his country he sacrificed his profitable interets, and gave his energies to the preservation of the Union. After an immense amount of difficulty, Colonel Frederick and his co-worker, Major McGibbon, working night and day, succeeded in enlisting enough loyal friends in and around St. Louis, to enable them to accomplish their purpose. By the middle of June three companies, and a nucleus of the fourth, was collected and rendezvoused at the St. Louis arsenal. Captains Hale, Renfrew, Veatch, and Elliott commanding.

About this time Captain S. W. Kelly was induced to become a recruiting officer, to assist in filling up the regiment. By the 24th of June he had recruited seventy men in his own neighborhood, and on that day an election was held, and S. W. Kelly was unanimously elected Captain, John Kelly First Lieutenant, and H. J. Maynard Second Lieutenant. On the 6th day of August, 1861, Captain Kelly numbered on the muster roll of his company, (F,) at the St. Louis Arsenal, seventy-one men; and through his influence three other companies had joined in the organization of the regiment. Captain Stookey, of Belleville, Ill., had recruited a large company of men for the service, and was now induced to join this regiment, thus making nine companies in rendezvous at the Arsenal on the 6th day of August.

As soon as the first three companies were formed, and before they were uniformed, they were sent down to Cape Girardeau, Mo., that place being threatened by the enemy, to assist in building fortifications. As soon as the next three companies were mustered in, and before they were uniformed, they were ordered to Pilot Knob, Mo. Here they underwent great hardship, not having uniforms or blankets, and scarcely anything to make them comfortable. The other three companies on their arrival at St. Louis, were sent with Colonel Frederick up the South-west branch of the Pacific railroad, to protect the bridges, etc., in order to keep that road open for the retreat of General Lyon's army after their defeat at Wilson's Creek, Mo. This work being accomplished, Colonel Frederick returned to St. Louis, and after overcoming many difficulties succeeded in getting the nine companies back to the arsenal. The next thing to be done, was to have them uniformed and drilled. This, also, was perseveringly and successfully attended to by the Colonel and Major McGibbon.

The men and the officers with one or two exceptions, were sadly deficient in a knowledge of military tactics or drills, and Colonel Frederick consequently took upon himself the task of drilling the regiment daily. In a short space of time he succeeded in making them quite well acquainted with company and battalion drills.

About the 1st of September 1861, Colonel Frederick and Major McGibbon, in order to promote the welfare of the regiment and secure good to the Union cause, tendered the command to Captain J. C. Kelton, then A. A. G. for General Fremont. Captain Kelton, after a time, accepted the command with the proviso that Frederick should have the Lieut. Colonelcy, and McGibbon the Majority. This arrangement was speedily confirmed by an election of the officers of the regiment, and the organization became complete,—one company only being required to make a full regiment. Upon Colonel Kelton assuming command, he procured the Tenth Company, viz. Company K, Captain Snyder, of Chicago, Ills., commanding, and this completed the Ninth Missouri, Volunteer Regiment.

Company K, was organized in the city of Chicago in

the month of September, 1861. A majority of the men were recruited by Lieutenant Abram J. Davids. It was originally intended as a company of sappers and miners, to be attached to Bissell's Engineer Regiment of the West. At least that was the inducement held out to the men. On the 5th of September the company was not quite full, and its services being needed immediately, forty-five men were taken from the Forty-Second Illinois, (then organizing at Chicago), and enrolled with the company on its muster into service on the 6th day of September, making an aggregate of ninety-seven men. Their camp equipage was drawn on the night of the 6th, and on the morning of the 7th marched under the command of Captain Henry N. Snyder, to the Chicago, Alton and St. Louis depot, and took the cars for St. Louis. They arrived at Illinoistown the evening of the same day, and in the morning crossed the Mississippi, and marched through St. Louis to Benton barracks; they here learned that they were to be attached to the Ninth Regiment Missouri Volunteer Infantry. It caused considerable dissatisfaction in the company, not that they had any objection to the regiment, but they wished to enter the arm of service for which they were recruited. Notwithstanding, there was no disobedience of orders.

On the 2d of September they were armed with Harper's Ferry rifles, and well equipped throughout; no company in the service ever started out better supplied with ordnance and camp equipage. On the afternoon of the 22d of September they left Benton barracks, marched to the depot, and took the cars en route for Jefferson City, where they arrived the next evening. They joined the Ninth Missouri on the following morning, and embarked with them on the steamer War Eagle, September 30th, bound for Boonville.

On the 22d of September, 1861, the regiment was ordered to Jefferson City, Mo., and on the 26th again ordered to Boonville, Mo. After remaining in camp a short time, Colonel Kelton was placed in command of a brigade, under General Pope. The brigade consisted of the Ninth Missouri, Lieut. Colonel Frederick, commanding; Thirty-Seventh Illinois, Colonel Julius White, commanding, and the Fifth Iowa, Colonel Worthington, commanding.

While at the St. Louis Arsenal, two companies under the command of Lieut. Colonel C. H. Frederick, were sent by Colonel F. P. Blair, up the Mississippi river to Howell's Island, where he captured five valuable steamboats from the hands of the rebels, who were about to use them to cross their forces to the south side, to join the rebel General Price. The total value of property thus secured from the hands of the rebels, amounted to two hundred and fifty thousand dollars. He also skirmished over the island in search of a rebel camp, and by this movement it was effectually broken up. Those two companies were composed of picked men from the different companies of the regiment.

HISTORY

OF THE

FIFTY-NINTH REGIMENT,

ILLINOIS VOLUNTEER INFANTRY.

CHAPTER I.

The Fifty Ninth Illinois Regiment entered the service of the United States, on the 6th day of September, 1861, under the cognomen of Ninth Missouri, at St. Louis, in that State. At that time the State of Illinois had filled her quota of volunteers, and would not receive the services of the patriotic young men who had collected themselves together for the purpose of preserving the glorious Union, then in danger of being severed.

The call of the President for seventy-five thousand volunteers, as well as that for forty-two thousand, had been so speedily filled by men whose business engagements, and perhaps entire want of business, permitted to enter the service without much sacrifice on their part, excluded, for the time being, these noble men from entering the service in the name of their own State. Although disappointed, they were still deter mined to devote their services to their country in some useful field of labor. Missouri was the most convenient and available State for this purpose, and was willing to accept of their aid, and hence the companies were organized into the Ninth Regiment of Missouri Volunteers, on the 6th of September, 1861.

General Fremont was in command of the department of Missouri, and as soon as the regiment was fully equiped, he ordered that it should report to General Pope, at Jefferson City, Mo. In the best of spirits the men left the old barracks and marched to the river for embarkation. The old and rickety steamer War Eagle lay in waiting, with steam up, to receive them. A very pleasant and lively time was passed in going up, and on their arrival at Jefferson City, a pretty camping ground received them, to await further orders. Here the regiment lay in camp until the 30th of September, when they were again embarked for farther up the river.

At Jefferson City the regiment was joined by a pioneer company of ninety-seven men, and by a squad of twenty men recruited by Captain Kelly, of company F, who fell into ranks as the regiment was re-embarking on the same old War Eagle, for "up the river."

The embarkation of a regiment, was, at that early day of the war, an exciting scene. Never before had such scenes been witnessed by the citizens of our inland river towns, nor had the men of the regiment ever before exhibited themselves to the gaze of the populace in such a display as they now did. The regiment was first marched in column down to the wharf, and ordered to stack arms. Then, as the way was open, one company at a time was marched to the boat and took quarters as directed. The quarters of each soldier consisted of just room enough to stand, or sit upon his knapsack on the floor, selected somewhere within the region of his own company. The regiment as it marched to the landing, to the time of the fife and drum, attracted the notice of the whole city. Its appearance was really captivating. The uniform being all new and unsoiled, and consisting of a closely fitting jacket of fine gray cloth, and pants of the same material, looked exceedingly neat and pleasing to the eye, and their knapsacks, cartridge boxes and guns, all new, and glistering in the sunshine, caused a sensation indescribable. No regiment has ever entered the service with more eclat than the Ninth Missouri. The men, wagons, horses and mules, all being huddled indiscriminately on board, the bell rang, and the old boat steamed up the turbid Missouri. During the night the boat rounded to at Boonville, Mo., and the regiment went into camp here for fourteen days, for the purpose of collecting supplies and fitting up for a campaign into the interior.

Boonville is a pretty town, of perhaps one thousand inhabitants, and is situated on the right bank of the Missouri River. It seems to be quite a flourishing place, and has something of an inland trade. The country in the vicinity is good and under good cultivation, and the improvements on the adjoining farms are excellent. The land is considerably broken, but very productive. It is a most splendid fruit country. No country in the world can produce larger and finer apples and peaches, than that around Boonville, as the soldiers of the Ninth can testify. It is also a fine grape region and can boast of many fine vineyards. Wine is made here to some extent, as the Ninth can also testify, for they had the pleasure of tasting some of it, as well as having plenty of fruit while in camp here. A majority of the citizens are professedly friends to the cause of the Union, and are disposed to treat the soldier kindly and with hospitality, so long, at least, as the

Union army is in the neighborhood. There are some who turn the cold shoulder and show a disposition to insult and annoyance, but they are more numerous in the country than in town, and this is more to our liking than otherwise; for it is but little we need from the citizens in town, but from the country we need mules, horses and forage, and confiscation is now the order of the day.

As soon as the regiment had comfortably arranged camp, a detail was made to go into the country prospecting for contraband stock. There were twelve or fifteen wagons to each regiment to be furnished with mules or horses, at the rate of six to a team. The boys were not many days in finding stock enough to supply the demand, and in doing so they found some amusement for themselves, and received many deep and bitter curses from the owners of the stock.

Some four miles down the river, lived a wealthy old rebel sympathiser, who possessed several mules and some fine horses, which the boys took a fancy to, and concluded they must have. The old gentleman stubbornly refused to give them up, and made threats to shoot any one who attempted to interfere with his property. The prospecting party were too few in number to catch the mules and bring them off, so they started one of their number to camp after reinforcements, while the others remained to guard the stock, and amuse the old secesh with some of their Union arguments. The old man, at first, seemed very uneasy, but after a time quieted himself so as to apparently enjoy the society of the boys very much. Thus time passed until night approached, and supper was announced. The boys partook of the bounties of the table, and again engaged the old gentleman in conversation, and thus the hours went by till bed time. An invitation to retire was proffered them, which they politely refused, preferring rather to bunk it on the floor, where they were, than to indulge the luxury of sheets and feathers. If the old gentleman entertained any suspicions of roguery on the part of the boys, he gave no indications of the fact, but quietly wished them a good night's rest, and withdrew to his own apartment for the night. About three in the morning, the reinforcements arrived from camp, and quietly proceeded to let out and drive the mules off to town, while the boys on guard bridled and saddled four good horses and joined the detachment. Early in the morning, the old farmer presented himself to Colonel Kelton with his complaints. Patiently the Colonel listened to him, and then gave him vouchers for his confiscated property, to be paid if he should prove himself a faithful, good citizen of the United States. Thus, in the course of ten days, was the wagons all supplied with good teams.

Other preparations for a campaign being nearly completed, the regiment was in daily anticipation of a move. The sick were sent to town to be left at hospital. Dr. H. J. Maynard, First Assistant Surgeon of the regiment, was assigned to the duty of fitting up quarters for their reception, and with energy of purpose and goodness of heart he performed the duty. Fifty of the regiment were unfitted to start on the campaign on account of sickness. There were many cases of measles. This disease had attacked some of the boys at Jefferson City; three of whom were left in hospital there. Many of the cases left in charge of Dr. Maynard, were critical, but by his kind care and good treatment, speedily recovered.

The regimient was now in good condition for a march, and the boys all anxious to try the realities of a campaign. The weather was delightful and the roads good. Price and his army was somewhere in the country, and every one desired to be after him. Drilling had been faithfully practiced since coming to Boonville, and the men began to feel like old soldiers in military tactics, and were confident if they could overtake Price he would be defeated, and the war in Missouri would be speedily terminated. Orders finally came to march, and on the morning of the 12th of October, all was hurry and confusion in preparation for the start. Tents were to be struck and the wagons loaded. Knapsacks were to be packed and comfortably fitted to the back; haversacks to be filled with plenty of rations; wild mules to be caught from the corral and hitched to the wagons; and last, though not least, pretty apple girls and wash women to be settled with before leaving. All was accomplished in due time, and about noon the brigade moved out.

Three regiments composed the brigade: the Ninth Missouri, the Fifth Iowa and the Thirty-seventh Illinois—three as good regiments as ever shouldered a musket. Colonel Kelton was in command of the brigade.

While in camp here, two boys who had joined the regiment at St. Louis, deserted, and were never heard of. Their names are now forgotten, as they should be, and they themselves are now perhaps, if living, no more than wandering vagabonds.

CHAPTER II.

On Sunday, the 12th day of October, 1861, the brigade bid adieu to the attractions and comforts of civilized society, for the long period of three years or during the war. Little did they think, as they marched through the streets of Boonville, that it would require three years of sacrifice for the government of the United States to put down so insignificant a rebellion as that which was now raging through its borders. They doubted not of the ability of our armies now in Missouri, to drive Price from the State, and restore peace in a few months. Their confidence in Fremont, in their own commanders and in themselves was unbounded. Their belief that the rebels would not withstand an equal contest, was well founded and did not diminish their ardor or their hopes of a speedy termination of the rebellion. They looked forward to a campaign of a few months duration, and then to a return to their homes, with peace attending them on the way. But how sadly were they to be disappointed! They supposed the policy upon which the war was to be conducted was fully established, and that all there was to do was to whip out the rebels, who were at this time in arms against them. They did not anticipate that time, as it passed, would develop new schemes and new policies until the whole became entirely revolutionized, and magnified into the most terrible rebellion the world ever witnessed. They did not think that while they were going to battle with the enemy in their front, the Government at Washington was changing its policy, so that instead of one they would have ten rebels to fight, and instead of a six months campaign they would have a five years war. They had read the closing words of the President's inaugural address, to-wit: "Physically speaking, we can not separate. We can not remove our respective sections from each other, nor build an impassable wall between them. A husband and wife may be divorced and go out of the presence and beyond the reach of each other; but the different parts of our country can not do this. They can not but remain face to face; and intercourse, either amicable or hostile, must continue between them. Is it possible, then, to make that intercourse more advantageous or more satisfactory after separation than before? Can aliens make treaties easier than friends can make laws? Can treaties be more faithfully enforced between aliens, than laws can among friends? Suppose you go to war; you can not fight always, and when, after much loss on both sides, and no gain on either, you cease fighting, the identical questions, as to terms of intercourse, are again upon you.

"To the extent of my ability I shall take care, as the Constitution itself expressly enjoins upon me, that the laws of the Union be faithfully executed in all the States. Doing this I deem to be only a simple duty on my part. I shall perfectly perform it, so far as is practicable, unless my rightful masters, the American people, shall withhold the requisition, or, in some authoritative manner, direct the contrary. I trust this will not be regarded as a menace, but only as the declared purpose of the Union, that it will constitutionally defend and maintain itself. In doing this there need be no bloodshed or violence, and there shall be none, unless it is forced upon the national authority. The power confided to me will be used to hold, occupy and possess the property and places belonging to the government, and collect the duties and imports. But *beyond what may be necessary for these objects, there will be no invasion—no using of force against or among the people anywhere.*

"In your hands, my dissatisfied fellow-countrymen, and not in mine, is the momentous issue of civil war. You have no oath registered in Heaven to destroy the government: while I shall have the most solemn one to preserve, protect and defend it." And they had all confidence in the promises of the President, that the "laws of the Union should be faithfully executed in *all* the States," and that the power confided to him would be used to "hold, occupy and possess the property and places belonging to the government, and collect the duties and imposts; but beyond what may be necessary for these objects, there will be no invasion—no using of force against or among the people anywhere." And they knew that Congress had voted, for the use of the President, one hundred thousand more men, and one hundred million more dollars than he had requested, to make the contest a short and decisive one," and they knew that that number of men was about "one-tenth of those, of proper age, within the regions where apparently all are willing to engage," and that the "sum is less than a twenty-third part of the value owned by the men who seem ready to devote the whole." Knowing these things, the members of the Ninth Missouri marched out from Boonville with light hearts and heavy knapsacks, without a murmur. They knew that

(2)

while they were under Fremont, they were entirely able to destroy every vestige of rebellion in Missouri. Over three hundred thousand soldiers, in other fields, were waiting orders from the Federal government, or were in active service; and that sixty odd vessels, with one thousand one hundred and seventy-four guns, were in commission, and twenty-three steam gun boats were on the stocks rapidly approaching completion, if not already completed. That sixty regiments of Federal troops were encamped near Washington, and that every armory in the land was at work night and day. Knowing all these things, why should they not anticipate a speedy termination to their soldier life, and enjoy in anticipation home society once more? Alas, little did they suppose that they themselves were to be the instruments in the hands of the President to work out the "salvation of the Almighty."

It is said that Governor Yates, of Illinois, telegraphed to the President at a certain time, to "call out one million of men, instead of three hundred thousand, that he might make quick work of the rebellion." The President replied: "Hold on Dick; let's wait and see the salvation of the Almighty." Had the President deemed it policy to have adopted Dick's advice, the rebellion might have been quelled, but perhaps the cause would not have been removed; and our good, honest President has not only been aiming to quell the rebellion, but to remove the cause at the same time. Hence the instrumentality of the army in establishing the policy of the administration. As the army progressed in strength and military discipline, so did the views of the administration and people change in regard to what might be accomplished in the destruction of the *causus belli*. And hence the "military necessities."

The brigade marched a few miles from town and bivouacked for the night. On the 13th and 14th it marched about twenty-eight miles, and went into camp near Syracuse.

The country is here not so broken as at Boonville, and is under good cultivation, with neat and comfortable farm houses and barns dotting the whole landscape.

The regiment lay in camp here on the 15th, and on the morning of the 16th, struck tents and took up the line of march for the rebel army. Price is reported to be about seventy-five miles to the south-west, erecting fortifications.

Since leaving Boonville, some of those who were indisposed on starting, had become so sick as to be unable to proceed, and were consequently taken to Syracuse, and left there to be disposed of by the Medical Director in charge. From Syracuse they were sent to St. Louis, to the hospital.

When leaving camp, the writer being detained until after the regiment had moved, came across a young man who had laid himself down by the road-side to die, as he said. He was taking the measels and was quite sick. The Surgeon of the regiment, Dr. Hazlett, had overlooked, or been deceived in the appearance of this young man at the morning examination, and had ordered him to march with the regiment. This he was unable to do, and would have been left by the road-side if he had not been accidently discovered. With some difficulty he was conveyed to Syracuse and left in hospital. The commander of his company was subsequently notified of his death in the St. Louis hospital.

CHAPTER III.

From the 16th to the 23d of October, the regiment continued its line of march daily. It moved in a south-western direction, crossing the Pacific railroad at Otterville.

Otterville is a small town on the railroad, near the right bank of the Lamoine river. It numbers from three to five hundred inhabitants, most of whom are very indifferent to the Union cause. No manifestations of rejoicing were shown on the approach of the noble men who were coming to protect them from the ravages of the rebel army; no stars and stripes were spread to the breeze as they came in sight, but every one manifested a coolness which indicated very distinctly in which direction their sympathies lay.

The country still continues to be very good. The farming lands are here under good cultivation and well improved. The soil is productive, and gives liberally into the hands of the cultivator. Every one seems to be prospering but somewhat discouraged at this time, as Price's army made rather heavy draws on their granaries and larders as he passed through here, and the Union army is now claiming a share of what they have left. There is yet an abundance to supply all demands, and no one need to suffer.

The brigade passes through Otterville without halting, and none but a few stragglers have any thing to say to the citizens, either to aggravate or soothe them. The direction taken is towards Warsaw, on the Osage river, where, it is rumored, Price is entrenching.

The routine of a campaign is now fully commenced. Reveille is sounded at five o'clock in the morning—all hands must then turn out to roll call—breakfast is cooked, and at seven the bugle sounds to fall in for the march. Two hours steady march follows, and then a rest of ten minutes, and *thus* until twelve or fifteen miles is passed over, when, if wood and water is convenient, camp is selected, tents are pitched, supper is provided, retreat is sounded, and all becomes quiet for the night. Thus it was with the Ninth, until their arrival at Warsaw. There is nothing to enliven the monotony of the march but the lively jokes and sallies of wit of the boys, and the change of scenery through which they pass.

The distance from Otterville to Warsaw, by the roads the regiment moved, is perhaps seventy miles, and the face of the country is considerably variegated. For the most part it is a level, unbroken region until you approach the bluffs of the Osage. The land is however rolling and enough diversified with hills and elevated peaks, to make it interesting to the traveler.

On the 23d of October, the regiment went into camp two miles north of Warsaw, to await the construction of a military bridge across the Osage river. The Osage at this point is about three hundred yards wide, with abrupt high banks and a deep swift current, so that it is impossible to cross an army in any other way than by means of a strong substantial bridge.

On the arrival of the division, as many "sappers and miners" and laborers as could be profitably employed, were set to work, and in forty-eight hours the bridge was ready for crossing. It was a very rude structure, but answered every purpose.

At Warsaw other troops came in from other directions, and swelled the forces which were to cross at this point to quite a large army. Some arrived in the morning before the Ninth, and about ten thousand passed the regiment after it had gone into camp. The weather continues delightful, and regiments coming in and passing, with their bright guns and accoutrements, present a splendid and most cheering spectacle.

There was great disappointment manifested by the troops on their arrival here and finding that Price was still on the wing. Here is where madame rumor had strongly entrenched the rebel army, and the boys had confidently expected to have a battle with him at this point. Their chagrin was great when they learned that he had still two or three weeks the start of them towards Arkansas. They were consoled somewhat by a probability that he might stop at Springfield and give them battle. They now felt that after being reinforced by so vast an army as seemed to have joined them here, they could whip the whole southern confederacy, before breakfast, some bright morning, if it could be found. Although disappointed, they were not discouraged, but were very eager for the pursuit to recommence.

While laying here those who could get passes, and some who could not, went over to town, and spent the day in making observations. Warsaw was the first town the boys had any leisure or opportunity to visit since leaving Boonville, and it was quite a treat for them to chat with the citizens, and partake of their hospitalities. A few of them came back to camp pretty blue,—something besides water having been found in Warsaw,—and a few did not return until the next morning, having found some other attractions to detain them.

Although there was quite a number of men reporting to the surgeon at the morning sick call, there were but few serious cases of disease in the regiment at this time. The seeds of the measles had produced its fruits and disappeared, and now the regiment was comparatively healthy. While laying here, news was received of the death of Johnson Kyle, of Company D, at Jefferson City. He was one of the three left there sick with the Measles, when the regiment started for Boonville. His name heads the list of deaths to be recorded by the regiment, after leaving St. Louis. John Burk, of Co. F, very soon followed him, and occupies the second place in that honored list.

CHAPTER IV.

On the morning of the 25th of October, the troops commenced crossing the river, and about 11 o'clock, A. M., the Ninth Missouri landed on the opposite shore, and halted an hour for dinner, and for stragglers to come up from Warsaw. Although orders against straggling was very strict, and the punishment threatened, severe, many of the soldiers fell out of ranks, and slipped off to town.

Warsaw is situated on the left bank of the Osage river, and is the largest town passed through since leaving Boonville. There being no towns of any size within many miles of it, it has quite an extended country trade, and boasts of several large stores and business houses of different kinds. The rebels while here, two weeks since, supplied themselves with goods to a large amount, from two or three Union Stores which were in the town. The merchants and citizens here are still undecided as to which cause they should give their influence. They are all, however, willing to be let alone. No demonstrations of satisfaction or the contrary, was manifested while the army remained here.

At 1 o'clock, the bugal sounded, and the line of march was again taken up and continued until the 30th, when the army went into camp for a day or two, at Humansville. The direction from Warsaw to Humansville, is southward, and the fear of the men now was, that the rebels were making for Arkansas. Rumor again had it that they were fortifying somewhere between here and Springfield, Missouri; but the boys did not credit it. Nothing reliable could be obtained of their whereabouts, and Arkansas appeared to be the most inviting place for a fleeing army. At any rate, it was evident that they had so far, fled as fast as they had been pursued.

The country from the Osage to this point is poor, broken and rocky. It seems as though nature intended this as the stone quarry for the universe. Here is stone enough to supply the United States with building material for centuries. The roads are all stone, the hills are solid rock, and the fields are stone. There is very little tillable lands south of the Osage, until within the vicinity of Humansville. There are a few farms, and occasionally a small town, but they are for the most part deserted. The inhabitants, perhaps, have gone south with Price. Quincy, the largest town on the road, is entirely deserted; the citizens all being rebels.

The only incident of note, during the march from the Osage, to Humansville, was the return to the army of Major White and his Prairie Scouts.

On the 30th of September, Price evacuated Lexington, and commenced a retreat to the south. He left a rebel guard there in charge of some Union prisoners. On the 15th of October, Major White, commanding a squadron of cavalry, called Prairie Scouts, with two and twenty men, made a forced march of nearly sixty miles, surprised Lexington, dispersed the rebels, captured sixty or seventy prisoners, took two steam ferry boats, and some other less valuable articles, secured the Union prisoners left there, and with a rebel captured flag, returned by another route to Warsaw, traveling with neither provisions nor transportation, and joining Freemont's forces south of the Osage. As characteristic of the energy of the men whom Gen. Freemont gathered about him, it is worth narrating, that Major White's horses being unshod, he procured some old iron, called for blacksmiths from the ranks, took possession of two unoccupied blacksmsith's shop, and in five days made the shoes and shod all his horses. At another time, the cartridges being spoiled by rain, they procured powder and lead, and turning a carpenter's shop into a cartridge factory, made three thousand cartridges. Such men could march, if necessary, without waiting for army wagons and regular equipments. As the Major and his Prairie Scouts proceeded to Head Quarters, they were greeted with cheer after cheer by the soldiers. The rebel flag, being the first they had seen, was a great curiosity to the boys. In contrast with their own loved stars and stripes, it was an insignificant affair. Its stars and bars elicited the scorn and contempt of every one who saw it. The curses bestowed upon it were not loud, but they were deep and came from the heart.

CHAPTER V.

On the 30th of October, the Brigade went into camp, near Humansville. Humansville, is a small town in Hickory County, Mo., and is the only place where any demonstrations were made, in honor of the stars and stripes, between Boonville and Springfield. Here the soldiers of the Union were welcomed by the waiving of flags and the smiles of the women, and the kindly greetings of the citizens generally. A portion of Price's army had passed through this place, some three weeks before, and had carried off all the goods belonging to the merchants, and had mistreated the inhabitants of the town and vicinity to such a degree, that they were heartily tired of their presence, and were rejoiced at the approach of the Federal troops.

The weather continues pleasant, and an opportunity is here offered the boys to wash up their clothing. This was rather an amusing task, as they had not as yet become accustomed to such work. Fires were started along the branches, and by the use of their camp kettles, they managed to hang out quite a respectable lot of clean *army linen*. Those having money and not being partial to the washing business, had their washing done by the women of the town, at the rate of ten cents per piece.

When going into camp it was thought that, perhaps, several days would be spent here, to allow the men some rest and to ascertain the distance to, and position of the enemy; but about noon of the 31st, orders came to be ready to march at a moment's notice.

The sick of the regiment, had been increasing for the last ten days, to such an extent, that now there was no means of conveying them any farther. Thus far, they had been transported in wagons, but it was now necessary to select such as could not, in a measure, provide for themselves, and leave them behind. The Surgeon, therefore, fitted up the Meeting-house in town, in the best possible manner, and removed the sick to it. A cook, some nurses, and several days rations, were left with them. Poor fellows! they all nearly starved to death before they could get away, and three did die from the effects of disease and want of proper nourishment. After the army left, the patriotism of the ladies and gentlemen of the town, oozed out at their fingers ends, and our sick boys could get nothing from them. One man, John Clemens, of Co. H, who was very sick when taken there, died on the 4th of November. Bromwell Kitchen, of Co. F, soon followed, and Nathaniel B. Westbrook, of Co. A, died on the 20th. The others eventually found their way to the regiment.

At 4 o'clock orders were received to strike tents and move out. An hour was now spent in busy preparation for the march. No one had thought that there would be a move before morning, and all were taken by surprise at the order to march just as night was setting in. Conjectures flew thick and fast through camp, as to what caused the haste in moving. Some supposed that Price was not far away, and that they were going to surprise him by a night attack. Some supposed one thing and some another, but all was wrapped in uncertainty.

At 6 o'clock, the bugle sounded to fall in, and the first night march of the regiment, now commenced. Camp was one and a half miles west of Humansville, and to get to the main road to Springfield, the regiment had to retrace its march back through the town. When therefore it commenced filing off in the direction it had come, the impression prevailed that they were on the retreat. Retreat! retreat, passed along the line, we are on the retreat—what does this mean, was the general inquiry. As soon, however, as they had passed through town, and struck the Springfield road, they found that they were not retreating, but were continuing their old line of march. This pleased them, and with alacrity they moved forward. The moon had not yet made its appearance, and the evening was quite dark. Several of the boys in going over the rough roads, fell and crippled themselves so as to be unable to proceed. The large stones which composed the road, would sometimes form steps of six inches in hight, and in stepping, they would fall forward with serious results. The moon now makes her appearance, bright and fair, and the road becomes distinct so that marching becomes easy, and much more rapid progress is made. The march continued till near morning, when the troops bivouacked for a few hours rest.

The bugle again sounds, and the march is continued. At 12 o'clock, a halt is again called, and an order is brought round to lighten baggage. All extra, useless and heavy baggage is ordered to be left, under guard, until brought forward by the wagon train. This is indicative of a forced march, or a going into battle. The latter is not probable, as no enemy is reported near. At 2 o'clock, the regiment moved out in light equipments.

Shortly after starting, a rumor got afloat that Price was really making a stand at Springfield. This news was received with a shout, and a more rapid movement of the troops. From this time until its arrival at Springfield, the regiment had no other than absolutely needful rest. The nearer the approach to Springfield, the more confirmed became the report of the rebel army being in that vicinity. The regiment having made ten or twelve miles this afternoon, went into camp on the banks of a small creek, which happened to run in the right place for their convenience.

Here an incident occurred which came very near terminating the life of one of the boys. He had gone to the creek to wash, and while there, walked out on a small log which projected from the bank over the water. His weight was too great for the support of the log; it gave way and he fell with his back across a log below him, and his head and shoulders into the water. He was badly hurt, and had there been no assistance near by, he would have drowned. He was unable to march for several days, so as to keep up with the regiment. The march from here to Springfield was uninterrupted, and on the night of the 3d of November, the regiment went into camp within easy distance of Springfield.

On the morning of the 5th, the Ninth Missouri found itself encamped on the out skirts of a large army Fremont had arrived with the greater portion of his army several days before, and driven Price from Springfield, and was now awaiting for the balance of his forces to come up. The Ninth had marched, in the last two days and nights, over fifty miles, to be in time for the anticipated advance, and they were now rejoiced that they had arrived in due season. A more happy set of men than those of the Ninth Missouri, could not have been found in the army. It had been on the march twenty days, with but little prospect of overtaking the enemy. Now the enemy were before them, and their march was perhaps terminated for the present.

CHAPTER VI.

On the approach of General Fremont, Price had fallen back to a chosen position, some ten miles south of Springfield, leaving a garrison of three or four hundred men to hold the place, until he could get thoroughly entrenched in his new position, and to give General McCullough time to join him from below, with his Texas and Arkansas forces.

General Fremont, in order to disperse this rebel garrison and get possession of the town, directed Major Zagonyi, commandant of General Fremont's body guard, to ride forward with a force of about three hundred, to make a reconnoisance, and, if practicable, capture or disperse the rebels, and take possession of the village. Major Zagonyi was a Hungarian officer, drawn to the western service by the fame of Fremont.

He had himself recruited the body guard which he commanded. It consisted of three companies of carefully picked men, armed with light sabers and revolvers. The first company also carried carbines. One hundred and sixty of this guard, with one hundred and forty of Major White's Prairie Scouts, already spoken of, constituted his force. As he advanced, he learned that the rebel guard had been reinforced, and that over two thousand men were ready to receive him. They had also been warned of his approach, and surprise was impossible. Prudence would have dictated that he return for reinforcements.

But Fremont's body guard had been a subject of much ridicule and abuse. He determined to make good its reputation for valor, at least. Perhaps by attacking the enemy in the rear, he might still secure the benefit of a surprise. This advantage he would gain, if possible. A detour of twelve miles around Springfield brought them to the rebel's position, but upon their south flank.

They were strongly posted just west of the village, on the top of a hill, which sloped toward the west. Immediately in their rear was a thick wood, impenetrable by cavalry. Before they came within sight of the enemy, Zagonyi halted his men. Drawing them up in line, he addressed them in the following brief and nervous words:

"Fellow-soldiers, this is your first battle. For our three hundred, the enemy are two thousand. If any of you are sick or tired by the long march, or if any think the number is too great, now is the time to turn back."

He paused; no one was sick or tired. "We must not retreat," he continued. "Our honor, and the honor of our General, and of our country, tell us to go on. I will lead you. We have been called holiday soldiers for the pavements of St. Louis. To-day we will show that we are soldiers for the battle. Your watchword shall be 'Fremont and the Union!' Draw sabre! By the right flank—quick trot—march!"

With that shout—"Fremont and the Union!"—upon their lips, their horses pressed into a quick gallop, they turn the corner which brings them in sight of the foe. There is no surprise. In line of battle, protected in the rear by a wood which no cavalry can enter, the rebels stand, forewarned, ready to receive the charge. There is no time to delay—none to draw back. In a moment they have reached the foot of the hill. The rebel fire sweeps over their heads. The Prairie Scouts, by a misunderstanding of orders, become separated from their companions, and fail to join them again. Up the steep hill the hundred and sixty men press upon the two thousand of their foe. Seven guard horses fell upon a space not more than twenty feet square. But nothing can check their wild enthusiasm. They break through the rebel line. They drive the infantry back into the woods. They scatter the hostile cavalry on this side, and on that. They pursue the flying rebels down the hill again, and through the streets of the village.

It seems incredible, yet it is sober history—not romance; in less than three minutes, that body-guard of a hundred and sixty men had utterly routed and scattered an enemy twenty-two hundred strong. Planting the Union flag upon the court house, they retire as night set in, that they may not be surprised in the darkness by new rebel forces. Their loss was sixteen killed and twenty eight wounded, out of the whole three hundred.

This has been pronounced an unnecessary sacrifice. The charge, it is said, was ill judged. But the bravery surely merits the highest commendation, and the success sanctifies the judgment of Zagonyi, which directed the assault. Moreover, we needed the example of this chivalrous dash and daring, to wake up some of our too cautious generals, and to inspire that enthusiasm and that confidence of success, which are essential to great accomplishments. For let it not be forgotten, that this was an expedition, which, in its ultimate results, was designed to sweep the Mississippi to the Gulf.

The ladies of Springfield, thus redeemed from rebel marauders, requested permission to present to their heroic deliver a Union flag. Will it be believed? When this body-guard returned to St. Louis, by peremtory orders from Washington, it was disbanded; the officers retired from service, and the men were denied rations and forage. It was deemed inexpedient that a corps should exist, so enthusiastically devoted to their chivalrous leader. In the order which came for their disbanding, they were condemned for "words spoken at Springfield." Condemned for that war-cry, which inspired to as glorious a charge as was ever made on battle field, "Fremont and the Union."

Zagonyi, in his official report of the battle, says: "Their war-cry, 'Fremont and the Union,' broke forth like thunder. Half of my command charged upon the infantry, and the remainder upon the cavalry, breaking their line at every point. The infantry retired into the thick wood, where it was impossible to follow them. The cavalry fled in all directions through the town. I rallied and charged through the streets, in all directions, about twenty times, returning at last to the court house, where I raised the flag of one of my companies, liberated the prisoners, and united my men, who now amounted to seventy, the rest being scattered or lost.

"From the beginning to the end, the body-guard behaved with the utmost coolness. I have seen battles and cavalry charges before; but I never imagined that a body of men could endure and accomplish so much in the face of such fearful disadvantage. At the cry of 'Fremont and the Union,' which was raised at every charge, they dashed forward repeatedly in perfect order, and with resistless energy. Many of my officers, non-commissioned officers and privates, had three, or even four horses killed under them. Many performed acts of heroism; not one but did his whole duty."

On the 29th of October, General Fremont established his head-quarters at Springfield. From Boonville to Springfield he had invariably marched with the advance of his army. On the 30th, General Ashboth brought up his division, and General Lane, on the same day, appeared with his brigade of Kansas border men, and two hundred mounted Indians and negroes. And on the 2d and 3d of November, General Pope brought up the rear with his command, of which the Ninth Missouri formed a part.

Since leaving Humanville, the health of the regiment continued good. Nearly all the men had been able to march up with the regiment. Those who gave out on the way were given passes by the Surgeon to fall back on the train and ride on the wagons. At this time there was but one ambulance allowed to each regiment, and this was used principally by the Surgeon for his own convenience, to the exclusion of the sick and disabled.

Ambulances had been provided, to move in the rear of the regiments on a march, and to attend them in time of battle for the purpose of transporting those who became disabled on the march, and for hauling the wounded from the battle field; but the Surgeons did not seem to understand it in that light. They took it for granted that ambulances were an especial comfort provided for themselves, and appropriated them accordingly. Many an anxious look is cast at the lazy Doctor, riding in the ambulance, by the sick, sore-footed soldier. Many a sick, weary and worn-out soldier is allowed to fall by the wayside, or to climb on the top of a loaded lumbering old army wagon, and ride with the hot sun pouring his ardent rays upon him, until night, or until the march is ended; while the healthy, robust Surgeon takes his ease in the closely covered and nicely cushioned ambulance.

The Surgeon is allowed two horses for his especial use, and now his lackey, detailed from the ranks, is riding one and leading the other behind the ambulance. The Surgeon has ridden on horse back during the cool of the morning, but now the heat is too oppressive and he retires to the shade of the vehicles, leaving his fat, sleek and magnificently caparisoned charger to be cared for by the unmanly soldier, who prefers being a lackey to wearing the honor and manhood of the man in the ranks.

The staff officers, and those of the line also, are allowed by government eleven dollars per month to pay servants for attending them, but as a general rule, they manage to get a soldier from the ranks to do their work, at the expense of the government, and put the eleven dollars into their own pockets. There are some men who scorn to stoop to such trickery; but it is a notable fact, that there are many, wearing the insignia of high official stations, who take advantage of their oath for the pitiful sum of eleven dollars per month. And it is also a fact, that there are men who have voluntarily taken upon themselves an oath to serve their country as good soldiers, who willingly allow themselves to be placed upon a footing with the veriest colored slaves in the land. The language is not too harsh. A soldier has been seen washing the feet and trimming the toe-nails of his captain, and this not only once, but habitually. The appellation given to him, and those of his calling, was "Toe-Pick."

CHAPTER VII.

On the morning of the 5th the regiment moved quarters to within a mile of town, and pitched their tents in regular camp order. The whole country for miles around Springfield was now filled with tents, and soldiers were as thick as ants on an ant hill. The whole army of Fremont was now here, and was said to number seventy-two thousand—or, there was said to be seventy-two thousand rations issued. A more noble looking set of men were never gathered into an army. Filled with enthusiasm and confidence in their leader, this army could not have been defeated by any rebel force brought against it. The men were very anxious for a forward move toward the enemy, and rumor had it that in a day or two the enemy would be met. But, alas! for human calculations. No movement was at this time to be made against the foe; but, instead, an inglorious retreat. Shame, and deathless infamy, attend the instigators of the retrograde movement of this splendid army.

On the 2d day of Movember General Fremont received notice of his recall to St. Louis to answer charges preferred against him, and of his being superceded in his command by General Hunter. Why was this retrograde movement to be made? Why was General Fremont removed from the command at this most auspicious moment? "Not until the secret *political* history of the rebellion, which unmasks hearts and exhibits motives, shall be written, can these questions be fully answered."

As soon as the intelligence that General Fremont was superceded by General Hunter spread through the camp, the wildest excitement everywhere prevailed. "Officers and men organized themselves into indignation meetings. Large numbers of officers declared their determination to resign. Whole companies threw down their arms."

General Fremont consecrated all his personal influence, entreating the men to remain, like true patriots, at their posts. He sent immediately to General Hunter the intelligence of his appointment, and, without delay, issued the following beautiful and effective appeal to the army:

"HEAD-QUARTERS WESTERN DEP'T.,
"SPRINGFIELD, Mo., Nov. 2d, 1861.

"SOLDIERS OF THE MISSISSIPPI ARMY:—Agreeably to orders this day received I take leave of you. Although our army has been of sudden growth, we have grown up together, and I have become familiar with the brave and generous spirits which you bring to the defense of your country, and which makes me anticipate for you a brilliant career. Continue as you have begun, and give to my successor the same cordial and enthusiastic support with which you have encouraged me. Emulate the splendid example which you have already before you, and let me remain, as I am, proud of the noble army which I had thus far labored to bring together Soldiers, I regret to leave you. Most sincerely I thank you for the regard and confidence you have invariably shown to me. I deeply regret that I shall not have the honor to lead you to the victory which you are just about to win; but I shall claim to share with you in the joy of every triumph, and trust always to be fraternally remembered by my companions in arms.

"J. C. FREMONT,
"Major-General U. S. A."

In the evening, one hundred and ten officers, including every brigadier-general in the army, visited General Fremont in a body. They presented him a written address, full of sympathy and respect, and earnestly urged him to lead them against the enemy. General Fremont replied to the address, that, if General Hunter did not arrive before morning, he would comply with their request. At eight o'clock in the evening he accordingly issued the order of battle. The enemy occupied the same ground as that which they had occupied in the battle of Wilson's Creek. General Lyon's plan of attack was to be substantially followed.

The rebels were to be surrounded. Generals Sigle and Lane were to assail them in the rear, General Asboth from the east, Generals McKinstry and Pope in front. The attack was to be simultaneous. Every camp was astir with the inspiriting news. Every soldier was full of enthusiasm.

But at midnight General Hunter arrived. General Fremont informed him of the condition of affairs, advised him of his plans, and surrendered the command into his hands. The order for battle was forthwith countermanded, and orders were issued to the army to prepare to turn their backs upon the foe, and retrace their march to St. Louis. The next morning General Fremont and his staff left the camp. As he passed along the soldiers crowded the streets and the roadsides to witness his departure, and, as they returned to their quarters, each one asked himself the question : "Why has Fremont been removed?" No ground for his removal had ever been made known. It was suggested that he was too extravagant in the financial management of his department. But there was no more justice in charging him with extravagance than there would have been any other General in command of a department. "Wherever there is carrion the vultures flock." Wherever there is an opportunity for public plunder corrupt men greedily gather. They abounded in Washington, in New York, in St. Louis; but no definite charges could be made that General Fremont ever participated in any scheme to defraud the Government. The mystery lay in the fact that General Fremont was far in advance of the nation's representatives, either in the field or cabinet. "He realized that the rebels were in earnest. He realized that all attempts at pacification by timidity and concessions to traitors were unavailing, and would but add fuel to the flame. He realized that the only way to stop rebellion was to chastise rebels with the rod of justice." And, realizing these things, he issued the following proclamation, which gave great offense to the more timid officials :

"HEAD-QUARTERS WESTERN DEP'T.
"ST. LOUIS, Mo., August 31st, 1861.

"Circumstances, in my judgment, of sufficient urgency, render it necessary that the Commanding General of this Department should assume the administrative powers of the State. Its disorganized condition, the helplessness of the civil authority, the total insecurity of life, and the devastation of property by bands of murderers and marauders, who infest nearly every county in the State, and avail themselves of the public misfortunes and the vicinity of a hostile force, to gratify private and neighborhood vengeance, and who find an enemy wherever they find plunder,—finally demand the severest measures to repress the daily increasing crimes and outrages, which are driving off the inhabitants and ruining the State. In this condition, the public safety and the success of our armies require unity of purpose, without let or hindrance, to the prompt administration of affairs.

"In order, therefore, to suppress disorder, to maintain, as far as now practicable, the public peace, and to give security and protection to the persons and property of loyal citizens, I do hereby extend, and declare established, martial law throughout the State of Missouri. The lines of the army of occupation in this State are, for the present, declared to extend from Leavenworth, by way of the posts of Jefferson City, Rolla and Ironton, to Cape Girardeau, on the Mississippi River. All persons who shall be taken with arms in their hands within these lines shall be tried by court martial, and, if found guilty, will be shot. The property, real and personal, of all persons in the State of Misssouri who shall take up arms against the United States, and who shall be directly proven to have taken active part with their enemies in the field, is declared to be confiscated to the public use; and their slaves, if any they have, are hereby declared free men.

"All persons who shall be proven to have destroyed, after the publication of this order, railroad tracks, bridges or telegraphs, shall suffer the extreme penalty of the law. All persons engaged in treasonable correspondence, in giving or procuring aid to the enemies of the United States, in fomenting tumult, in disturbing the public tranquility, by creating and circulating false reports or incendiary documents, are in their own interest warned that they are exposing themselves to sudden and sure punishment.

"All persons who have been led away from their allegiance are required to return to their homes forthwith; any such absence without sufficient cause will be held to be presumptive evidence against them.

"The object of this declaration is to place in the hands of the military authorities the power to give instantaneous effect to existing laws, and to supply such deficiencies as the conditions of war demand. But it is not intended to suspend the ordinary tribunals of the country, where the law will be administered by the civil officers in the usual manner, and with their customary authority, while the same can be peaceably exercised.

"The Commanding General will labor vigilantly for the public welfare, and in his efforts for their safety, hopes to obtain not only the acquiescence but the active support of the loyal people of the country.

"J. C. FREMONT,
"Major-General Commanding."

"An out-cry from all pro-slavery *partisans*, in all parts of the country, went up against the man who had first dared to proclaim liberty to the slaves of rebels." A demand was made for his removal. Fair means were not alone used for this end. The most strenuous efforts were secretly made to undermine him in the confidence of the Administration, and by bitter public attacks through the press to rob him of the confidence of the people. And success attended those efforts.

The President, whose duty it was to hold a controlling influence in the councils of the nation, coincided with this intriguing faction against his better judgment, and submitted to this great injustice—injustice both to Fremont and the country. The proclamation of General Fremont was accordingly modified, and Fremont himself deprived of his command.

On the reception of the President's letter, requesting him to modify his proclamation, Fremont replied:

"If," said he, "your better judgment decides that I was wrong in the article respecting the liberation of slaves, I have to ask that you will openly direct me to make the correction. The implied censure will be received as a soldier always should receive the reprimand of his chief. If I were to retract of my own accord it would imply that I myself thought it wrong, and that I had acted without the reflection which the gravity of the point demanded. But I did not. I acted with full deliberation, and with the certain conviction that it was a measure right and necessary, and I think so still."

General Fremont submitted to the modification, which was to confine the confiscation and liberation of only such slaves as had been actually employed by the rebels in military service. If they worked the guns they were to be free. If they only raised the cotton which enabled the rebels to buy the guns they were not to be free, but to be returned to their masters if they should escape to our lines in search of freedom. But this did not satisfy those who were even more anxious to treat the rebels with conciliation and have Fremont removed and his influence destroyed, than to strike the rebellion with heavy blows. Let Fremont be removed at all hazards. He was removed, and his army was recalled from Springfield, and in less than six months another army under General Curtis, pursuing the same plan which General Fremont had formed, and governed by the very policy recommended in his proclamation, marched over the same ground, under much more adverse circumstances, and met the enemy only after a tedious pursuit of one hundred and twenty miles farther off than the fall before.

On the morning of the 4th of November Abraham C. Coats, of Company C, was brought into the regimental hospital in an entirely unconscious condition. He was taken in the night with what was supposed to be a conjestive chill. Every means known to the Surgeon was resorted to to restore him to consciousness and preserve his life, but all were unavailing. He never spoke after being brought in, and died about noon of the next day. A *post mortem* examination revealed nothing to indicate the cause of his death.

Several of the boys were taken sick while in camp here, and when the regiment marched they were loaded into an army wagon to be transported to wherever the regiment might be destined. One of these died in the wagon the second night after leaving Springfield and was buried by the roadside. The others, after eight days' torture, arrived, more dead than alive, at Syracuse, where they remained in hospital all winter.

CHAPTER VIII.

On the morning of the 9th of November, with sad hearts and elongated countenances, the Ninth Missouri Volunteers took up the line of march, which they had so lately spun out in such glorious anticipations, to wind it back to the very place from whence they had started one month before.

The weather still continued fine, but the roads had become so awful dusty, that suffocation threatened to be the fate of every one who traveled them. There had been no rain since leaving Boonville. Water was becoming scarce, excepting in the larger streams; although Missouri is usually abundantly supplied with that refreshing element. Abundant crystal streams of purest water; springs bubbling from many a creviced rock and wells of unfailing depths, are met with every where in southern Missouri.

The regiment followed its old line of march, until after crossing the Osage, when it took the most direct road to Otterville. From Otterville it continued down the railroad to Syracuse, where it arrived on the 17th of November, having marched from Springfield in eight days, without rest. In its devious course from Boonville to Springfield, and from Springfield to Syracuse, the regiment had marched over three hundred miles.

On arriving at Syracuse, it bivoucked on a common in town, in anticipation of taking the cars in a day or two for St. Louis. Rumor had it, that the troops were all going to St. Louis, either to go into winter quarters or to be sent South. No one thought of wintering at Syracuse.

There was no enemy within one hundred and fifty miles of this place, and a necessity for stopping here did not exist. Yet, in this vicinity were they destined to lay in idleness for three long months.

As the regiment passed Warsaw, on its return, some of the boys, who had learned the working of the wires on their previous visit, again slipped from the ranks and succeeded in getting their canteens filled with the ardent. Two of these, on coming into camp just in the dusk of the evening, caused quite a sensation. They had been "hale fellows well met," until whisky had got advantage of their better judgment, when they agreed to disagree, and the one using the breech of his gun, as the strongest argument he could think of, knocked the other over the head with so severe a blow as to cause insensibility. A crowd was soon collected, and the belligerent one was placed under guard, while the defunct was hurried to the hospital, to be placed in hands of the Surgeon. On examination, the Surgeon discovered something of a cut on the scalp, which was bleeding pretty freely; and having a little too much of the ardent in his own hat to see single, he pronounced the man mortally wounded, with a fractured skull.

After having the bruise dressed, the Surgeon retired to his own quarters, leaving the impression that the man would not live through the night; in fact he gave it as his opinion, that he was in *articuls mortis* at this moment.

The commander of the regiment placed the one who gave the death-blow, under double guard, binding his hands and feet so as there should be no possibility of escape. By and by all retired to their quarters, and none, except the guard and the watchers by the side of the dying man, were awake in camp. The man lay very quiet until about eleven o'clock, when he was observed to draw a very heavy and prolonged inspiration. Soon another followed, and his eyes opened. For a moment they wandered restlessly over the tent, and then he sprung to his feet.

"Well! where the hell am I? What does this mean? Say, what is the meaning of this? Is this the hospital? How is it that I am here? I'm not sick. There is nothing the matter with me; where is my quarters, say, I am not going to stay here, that's certain!" and off he started like a quarter horse for his company.

The mystery was, that he was very much intoxicated when he was hit, and the blow only set him into a most profound drunken slumber. Early the next morning the Colonel released the prisoner, and the Surgeon passed the joke in good spirits, although his reputation in prognosis was somewhat impaired by the incident.

CHAPTER IX.

On the arrival of the regiment at Syracuse it was discovered that about fifty of the men were on the sick list. Some were quite sick from the effects of the continued jolting they had suffered in the wagons, while others were only worn down by hard marching.

The Surgeon immediately took possession of the Planter House, a deserted hotel in town, and established his hospital in it. Straw was procured, and the men were as comfortably placed upon it over the floor as circumstances would admit.

On the morning of the 18th the regiment was moved out two miles from town, and went into regular camp.

As the men were marching through the town the rain descended in torrents, wetting them thoroughly. This was the first rain seen since leaving Boonville, and was received in high glee.

Visions of St. Louis now began to grow dim in the eyes of some of the men, although many still believed that they were only waiting transportation. The Surgeon delayed, from day to day, making any provisions for the comfort of the sick, expecting orders to ship them for St. Louis. But orders never came, and it became a fixed fact that the regiment was to winter here.

Newspapers were brought to Syracuse daily, and something of what was going on in the world could be learned from them. During the last month a newspaper had not been seen in the regiment. Some of the officers would occasionally get a paper, but the soldiers never. From these it was ascertained that the war was still progressing, and that the rebellion was assuming a magnitude of unexpected dimensions.

Many of the soldiers were led to believe, by their withdrawal from Springfield, that their services would not much longer be required in the field, and that they would soon be allowed to go home, but on reading the papers they lay aside all such pleasing ideas.

The weather was now becoming quite cool, and tents were more carefully pitched than usual—ditches were dug, and embankments thrown up, to keep the cold winds from blowing in under them. Good warm blankets were issued, and a new suit of clothing provided, so that, so far as possible, suffering might be prevented. Plenty of wood was provided, and on cold days large fires were burning in front of every tent. At night pans of living coals were taken into the tents as substitutes for stoves. Thus they managed to keep quite comfortable. Army rations were in abundance, and the citizens were liberal in their supply of cakes, pies and apples, at a moderate compensation, and sometimes without any pay whatever. Occasionally one would come into camp more greedy of gain than his neighbor, or, perhaps, tinctured a little with secession proclivities; in such cases "confiscation" was the word, and his load would soon disappear, without his being any the richer.

The sick men, who were left at Boonville under the care of Doctor Maynard, now joined the regiment. Without an exception, the kind care and judicious treatment of this excellent Surgeon had restored all to good health, and they joined the regiment in good spirits, and were welcomed most cordially by their comrades.

About the 10th of December the regiment broke camp here and moved out to the bottoms of the Lamoine river. The object of the move was the erection of fortifications for the defense of the railroad bridge across the Lamoine. Their camp was selected on some swamp-bottom lands on the left bank of the river. The boys were immediately set to work cutting the trees and cleaning off the grounds, while details were sent off to work on the fortifications on the opposite bank of the river.

On the morning of the 14th marching orders were issued for the next day, and on the 15th, through a heavy snow storm, they marched to Sedalia, twenty-five miles distant. The roads were bad, and the marching very heavy, yet most of the men came into camp with the regiment. They were marched out for the purpose of cutting off recruits and a large supply train going to Price's army. When they arrived at Sedalia the work was being accomplished by another portion of the Division. A part of Davis' Division had taken another route, and had succeeded in overtaking and capturing some seventy wagons and one thousand one hundred prisoners, among whom was the son of the old General. The Ninth Missouri consequently had nothing to do but march back to its camp on the Lamoine. This it was two days in accomplishing. Thus marching fifty miles in three days. Thus making in all, since leaving Boonville, fully four hundred miles. Here the regiment remained until the 25th of January, 1862.

When the regiment removed from Syracuse to the Lamoine, the Surgeon, Doctor Hazlett, went with them, leaving sixty sick men at Syracuse in charge of the

Hospital Steward, without having made any preparations yet for their comfort. The building was very well calculated for an hospital, but needed renovating very badly, and should have had bunks built for the patients to lay on; but nothing of the kind had been attended to; and now, to attend to the wants of sixty sick men, only one nurse, one cook and the Steward, were to be had. Many of the men were desperately sick, and should have had better care taken of them; but, fortunately, only two cases proved fatal after the Surgeon left—Henry Rue, of Company F, on the 1st day of January, 1862, and John Rule, of Company D, on the 28th of the same month. Two also died while the Surgeon was in attendance—Boston Cherrington, of Company A, and McClenning, of Company E. At the Lamoine, Phillip Shindola, of Company B, James Edwards, Company C, George W. Lewis and William St. George, Company B, and William S. Gore, Company F, were taken sick, and died in January, 1862.

The living at the Hospital consisted of beef, pilot-bread, sugar and coffee or tea.

There was an hospital fund of money, accumulated by the commutation of rations belonging to sick men; but, as with the ambulances, the Surgeons are sometimes dishonest enough to appropriate this fund to their own use. The cooking facilities about the hospital consisted in a camp-kettle, (holding about five gallons,) for coffee or tea, and one of the same size for boiling beef, and a log fire out of doors. With these facilities the cook prepared the rations for sixty sick soldiers for over two months, rain, snow or shine, as the case might be.

The manner of feeding the patients was thus: The kettle of coffee and soup is brought into the center of the room where the sick are, and tin-cups are filled and handed round, and a "shingle" (pilot cracker) is handed at the same time, with a piece of boiled beef on it. If the patient has had money he has perhaps provided himself with a biscuit or piece of light bread, purchased of some citizen. The men set around over the floor on their straw pallets, and eat, some swearing at the coffee, and some cursing the soup, and all making some remark or other about the fare. One, for instance, would like some potatoes or chicken soup; one some bread and milk, one some corn bread, and another would fancy mush and milk. Sometimes these things could be procured by paying their own money for them, and thus there would be a feast. Poor fellows! They deserve better things than these, but it is impossible for the Steward and attendants to provide anything more suitable. May God forgive those who should look after these things for neglecting their duty, or for being dishonest.

The soldier in camp lives very similar to this: Messes are formed from the occupants of one tent, perhaps numbering four or five, or more; the rations are drawn, and all cooked in the same vessels. A small camp-kettle supplies them with coffee, and a larger one with boiled beef, bean-soup, etc. Then, with tin-cups, tin-plates, knives and forks, they pitch in, each one helping himself until he is satisfied. While eating he either stands or sits on the ground, as he may elect. Thus they live day after day and month after month and no variety unless they buy and pay for it themselves. Many of them *do* spend all their wages in buying something to eat. It is amusing to look through the streets of Syracuse, and see the soldiers buying the *luxuries* that the farmers' wives bring to town to sell.

Here are several wagons, surrounded by soldiers, buying and trying to buy, sausage meat, fresh pork, chickens, butter, eggs, pies, cakes, corn-bread, milk, apples, etc. The argus eyes of the ladies are kept busy, or else they make small profits. While many are honestly paying for what they get, others are playing confiscation, and dishonestly getting what they do not pay for. Pies and cakes are in great demand; and such pies! The pie-crust is made by wetting some flour with water until it becomes pasty, some sour apples are then wrapped up in it, and it is then dried in a moderately heated oven. When it is sufficiently done it can't be broken, but must be twisted asunder and swallowed in mass; yet the soldiers pay a quarter for such pies, and consider them a luxury.

The first case of bushwhacking known to the regiment occurred at Syracuse. A boy belonging to the Eighth Indiana Regiment was on his way to join his regiment, and stopping at the hospital to ascertain where he would find it, was induced to stay a day or two before going farther. The day following he walked out into the brush, about one hundred yards from the hospital, and was shot down by some unseen hand. The report of the gun was heard at the hospital, and in a few moments the body was found, laying on the snow, in a dying condition. There was an inch or two of snow on the ground, and it was thought the murderer might be found by his foot-prints in the snow. Several of the boys from the hospital started immediately in pursuit. The afternoon was spent in following foot marks through the woods, but nothing definite was ever learned of who committed the murder. One of the scouts reported on his return that "the scoundrel would never shoot another soldier," intimating that he had overtaken and shot the bushwhacker; but credit was not given to his story.

Toward the latter part of January, 1862, a post hospital was established at Otterville, near the Lamoine, and Dr. Hazlett, Surgeon of the Ninth Missouri, was appointed Post Surgeon. Dr. Maynard, in consequence, was relieved at Boonville, and, greatly to the satisfaction of the boys, took charge of the regiment. The Regimental Hospital Steward being yet at Syracuse, Dr. Maynard requested the Colonel of the regiment to order him to report to him for duty, as his presence was more needed at the regiment than at the hospital. The patients at Syracuse were about being removed to Otterville.

From this request of Doctor Maynard resulted a decision which may be of importance to many hospital stewards in the army. Many young men receive the appointment of hospital steward without knowing or inquiring to whom they are responsible for their good conduct, or whose orders they are in duty bound to obey. Hence they are imposed upon by the surgeons, and are made nothing less than menials for those vampires of the Government. On the request of Doctor Maynard, Lieutenant-Colonel Frederick, commanding the regiment, issued the order desired. On the same day Doctor Hazlett, Surgeon of the regiment, issued a similar order for the Steward to report to him at Otterville for duty. The decision in the case was, that "the Steward was subject only to the orders of the commanding officer of the regiment." This decision has since been confirmed. A hospital steward is not a surgeon's orderly.

Rumor now prevailed that the regiment would leave the Lamoine in a short time, and outside movements tended very much toward confirming the rumor. The sick were all ordered to Otterville; the hospital stores were inspected and reported, and any deficiency in the supply was ordered to be filled. There was, however, no want of hospital supplies at this time, thanks to the ladies of Wisconsin.

A delegation from those charitable ladies had, but a few days before, visited the army, with a large quantity of comforts, quilts, drawers, shirts, handkerchiefs, and magazines and newspapers, which they distributed to hospitals at the towns, and to the regiments, with liberal hands. God will abundantly bless the ladies of Wisconsin. When they have forgotten that their hands had prepared these inestimable presents for the soldier, his prayers will be ascending in their behalf. The death-bed of the soldier is made comfortable by the thoughtful liberality of these kind friends, and their hearts go out in thankful praises and gratitude to the fair donors.

CHAPTER X.

Orders were received by the regiment, on the morning of the 23d, to be ready to march at 8 o'clock, on the morning of the 25th, with three days rations in the haversack of each soldier.

The morning of the 25th of January, 1862, made its appearance, clear and cold, and found the regiment in marching trim. Some of the boys would have preferred waiting a day or two, as they were expecting a large supply of good things, from home. Some companies had already received their boxes of pies, cakes, turkeys, butter and et ceteras; but one or two other companies had failed to receive theirs, and were looking for them by every train. Letters had informed them of their being on the way, and the boys were starving to have them arrive; but there was no help for it, they must march and leave their 'goodies' for some one else to devour. It was too bad to so disapppoint the kind good friends at home, and still worse to be so disappointed themselves. There was no use of lamentations. At 8 o'clock the bugle sounded to fall in, and the troops moved out. The direction taken, was down the railroad, towards Syracuse; but before night, Syracuse was left in the rear, and Tipton, a small town six miles farther east, was approached. Here the regiment went into camp for the night. Early the next morning, the regiment crossed the railroad, and moved in a southerly direction, leaving all hopes of going to St. Louis, at Tipton. While on this day's march, an amusing incident occurred, showing conclusively in which direction the feelings of the soldier inclines.

One Moore, a citizen of Syracuse, with his overseer, came riding along by the regiments, in search of one of his slaves. The negro had disappeared from Syracuse, the day before, and old Moore had rightly suspected that he had joined the army. The Ninth Missouri, happened to be the regiment he was with. On discovering the boy, old Moore rode up to him, and ordered that he mount behind the overseer and ride back to town. The soldiers soon crowded around between the negro and his master, and ordered the latter to leave. The old gentleman did not incline to do so, without taking his negro with him. But the threats and threatening attitude of some of the boys, gave him to understand that he was not safe in remaining, and concluding that discretion was the better part of valor, he began an inglorious retreat, which at first was slow and reluctant; but as missiles of different kinds began to increase in thickness, his own speed increased accordingly, until him and his man Friday, disappeared under a sharp run of their horses. Nothing more was ever heard of old Moore, but his negro continued a good servant in the regiment, for more than a year.

The march was now continued through a very wild and broken region of country, with very bad roads and stormy weather, until the 2d day of February, when the Osage river was again to be crossed.

The regiment went into camp, on the left bank of the Osage, on the afternoon of the 2d, during a heavy snow storm. The weather had been stormy, ever since leaving Syracuse, and here it culminated in a cold driving snow storm. No one who has not experienced the trial, can imagine how disagreeable it is to go into camp under such circumstances as now surrounded the army. Rainy weather can be endured, and even enjoyed, as was proven on this march; but cold snowy weather is very trying to the nerves.

One evening the regiment went into camp, on a low piece of meadow land, near the Gravoi creek, after marching in the rain all day. They were wet, muddy and hungry. Orders had been issued to burn no rails on this march, under severe penalties. But here there was no other wood convenient, and the question with the boys was, how are we to make coffee? Twilight was consumed in trying to find something to start a fire with, but without success. As soon as darkness became visible, the rails began to move from the fence enclosing the meadow, and in half an hour thereafter, most genial and glowing fires were burning in all directions. Owing to bad roads, the camp equipage did not come up till towards morning, consequently there was no tents to pitch, and the entire night was spent by many of the boys, in dancing and whooping around the fires, in seemingly the most perfect enjoyment, although it rained in torrents. The next morning disclosed the fact that the meadow was all out-doors.

The question now arose, "how is the river to be crossed?"

"Look yonder," says a boy pointing down the river. "Yonder's a steamboat."

A steamboat on the Osage river! This was a surprise, no one had thought of crossing the river on a steamboat, but it seems that small boats had occasionally made their trips up to this point, and now one was here expressly to assist in crossing the army. She was just getting up steam, and pretty soon the troops commenced crossing. While the troops were crossing on the boat, the trains and artillery were crossing on a military bridge, constructed for the purpose. By noon of the 4th, the whole command was in camp, on the right bank of the river.

The troops lay here on the 5th to rest. The town, at the mouth of Sinn creek, is mostly deserted, the citizens being mostly rebels. The wealthiest and most respected one among them, is a Union man, and has given his money and influence freely, in support of the Government. A few weeks ago, he had a very large store here, and was doing an extensive business, but a squad of rebel Jayhawkers, visited him, and nearly robbed his store of all its goods. A remnant only was left. These were purchased by 'our' boys, now, at their own price, which was not at a great profit to the owner. The owner is now absent, and our boys do their own clerking. Hats, caps, tobacco, and cigars, seem to be most ready sale. Here the boys also procured some excellent cherry-bounce, on which they had a real jollification.

On the 6th, the line of march was taken up, and continued towards Lebanon, where the regiment arrived on the evening of the 7th. These were two days heavy marching, making fourteen miles on the 6th, and sixteen miles on the 7th, on very hilly and muddy roads. It is called seventy-five miles from here to Syracuse; but in coming, the regiment had marched some days twelve miles, and were at night, only five miles from the place of starting. Thus making at least, eighty-five miles in ten days marching, through the most inclement weather, and over the worst possible roads.

The regiment went into camp, a few miles west of Lebanon, and lay by on the 8th and 9th, to await the arrival of more troops.

While laying here, John Baker, of Company F, died, and was buried in the grave yard at Lebanon.

The 9th, is the Sabbath day—a day appointed and established among christians for public worship, and as a day of rest from labor; but among the 5,000 men that are here, very few are aware that it is Sunday, or a day of rest.

The fife and drums are playing and beating as lively, as on any week day, and the men are as busy drilling as they were through the week days, in regular camp. It is the first sunny day for two weeks, and hence the lively appearance of camp. A brass band is discoursing sweet music, over towards Lebanon, which can be heard very distinctly by the Ninth, and some of the boys are enjoying its melody, instead of participating in the hilarity of those around them.

A sham battle is to be fought this afternoon, in anticipation of a real one, which is expected to be had with the enemy, in a few days. Price is reported to be fortifying himself, seventeen miles this side of Springfield, which is about thirty miles from here. The battle has been decided, and now preparations are being made for an early march in the morning.

While laying here, a gentleman and lady, of African descent, who had been with the regiment since leaving St. Louis, concluded that they would retire from the army, to the shades of private life. The man had gained the confidence of the boys, and on leaving, they placed in his hands a considerable sum of money, to be given to their friends at home. One man gave him a good horse, to take for him, to St. Louis. He departed, and so the money and horse departed with him, and neither was ever heard of afterwards. The temptation was too great for a negro's cupidity.

CHAPTER XI.

On the morning of the 10th, the army was again on the move, the Ninth Missouri bringing up the rear of Jeff. C. Davis' division. The roads were very bad, but the weather was favorable, and the country more level than from Syracuse here. The sick and much extra baggage was left at Lebanon, to be brought up at a more convenient season.

It was now anticipated that the enemy would be attempting to impede the advance of our army, but no indications of their presence was discovered until the evening of the 12th. About one o'clock, of the 12th, General Sigel's column, which was advancing on another road, some half mile to our left, came upon their out-posts pickets, and a sharp skirmish ensued. As soon, however, as a piece of artillery could be brought to bear upon them, they fled in confusion, leaving the road undisputed. This was the first firing of artillery the Ninth Missouri had ever heard, and it caused a general excitement. The army halted about four o'clock, in a good position, and several companies from the different regiments were sent out through the woods as skirmishers. Companies F and A of the Ninth, was ordered to scout the woods for a mile or two in front. They were very proud of the distinction, and elicited the envy of the other companies. With erect and martial step, those two companies—the one, (company F.) commanded by Captain Kelly; the other, (company A.) by Captain Hale—filed off into the woods in search of the hidden foe. The boys in camp listened anxiously for the report of fire arms, and soon, in the distance, several volleys of musketry announced that the enemy had been found.

On the return of our skirmishers in the morning, they reported, that before they had advanced over half a mile, they heard firing in their front, and that Major Black, commanding the skirmishers, ordered an advance on double quick. The underbrush was thick and intensely dark, but by strenuous efforts the men succeeded in reaching an open space and getting into line of battle, just as the rebels began to disappear in an inglorious retreat. Some five hundred rebels had made a vigorous attack upon our cavalry pickets, (First Missouri,) but had been handsomely repulsed, with a loss of five killed and thirteen wounded, before the infantry could come up.

Before going out, many of the boys took the precaution to leave their money and valuables in the hands of their friends, so that if they should be killed or captured, their effects would be safe.

Early on the morning of the 13th, the army was again in motion. Springfield was now only seventeen miles distant, and no fortifications were yet discovered. Price is now known to be at Springfield, and he must either fight or run within the next forty-eight hours.

The army proceeded to within five miles of Springfield without any indications of the enemy; but now coming to an open country the troops were halted, and a long line of battle was formed across a very large piece of meadow land. The line was formed in front of some heavy timber skirting the meadow, and the supposition was that the enemy was posted in the timber, ready for battle. The troops marched into line on double quick, and in splendid style. The Ninth Missouri, led by its noble commander, Lieut. Colonel C. H. Frederick, now had an opportunity of displaying its proficiency in rapidity of action, and fell into line with the precision of veterans. Very soon the whole line was formed, and the men standing on their arms awaiting further orders. General Curtis and staff now rode along the line, with the announcement that Springfield was in our possession. Price had evacuated without a fight. The news was received with a shout and the tossing of hats in the air, mingled with curses and maledictions. Although it was pleasing news, yet the disappointment in not getting satisfaction out of the infernal scoundrels, was great among the troops. The line of battle was now broken and the troops again formed into marching order. And now commenced the most wonderful retreat and pursuit of two opposing armies, that the world had ever witnessed.

Price commenced the evacuation of Springfield on the 12th, and in four hours after the rear of his army had left the town, our advance was passing through in pursuit. It was said by the rebel sympathisers in town, that Price would make a stand at Wilson's Creek, ten miles below town; that he had twenty thousand fighting men, and would drive Curtis as he had General Lyon the summer before. It was more than probable that the rebel army numbered at least that many, if not more. Price had returned from Lexington to Springfield, on the 23d of December, 1861, with his whole army, and had been using all his energies to recruit and fill up his army until now. "He began to raise fifty thousand men for the Southern Confederacy,.

(5)

the object of which was to secure him the commission of Major General in the Southern Confederacy. He soon accomplished his object.

The men are sworn into the service for twelve months. Several regiments of the State Guard were soon broken up; they went into it very readily, because they were made to believe that as soon as Price was promoted, he would have power to order troops from any of the Southern States, and that they would soon make a clean thing of it in Missouri, and also invade Kansas and leave it as the Lord made it, without a house to shelter Jayhawkers. These men felt confident that they would soon be let loose to accomplish this glorious work, and were highly delighted with the idea, but the poor fellows were badly fooled." General Curtis and his brave boys were now rather interfering with their glorious anticipations.

The army made no delay in passing through town, but marched about three miles beyond, before going into camp. Camp was pitched on a large farm belonging to an old rebel, and his effects had now fallen into unsparing hands. The old gentleman had left a large, fine house, large barn and good log stable on his premises. The log stable was designed and worked up into quite a strong fort for the protection of the house and barn. Heavy timbers and earth were so thrown together as to be a perfect defence against musket balls, and port holes were opened for the use of the besieged. But they dare not use it at this time, and our boys soon made it untenable in the future. Soon after dark the house and barn afforded plenty of light to see to go to bed by, all over camp. Every thing about the premises was destroyed. The next morning ashes and embers alone marked the spot where the house and barn stood;

and posts and bottom rails indicated where fences had been.

On the 14th the march was continued to Wilson's Creek, for dinner, and several miles beyond for camp. Wilson's Creek is the scene of General Lyon's defeat and death, and the writer can do no better than transcribe, from Abbott's History of the Civil War in America, an account of the whole affair:

Wilson's Creek is a tributary of White River. From the village of Springfield, there is one road leading to Fayetteville, Arkansas, running in a south-westerly direction. Another road pursuing a course nearly due west, conducts to Mount Vernon. Along the banks of Wilson's Creek there is a cross road, which connects the Fayetteville and the Mount Vernon roads. The valley of this creek is about twenty rods in width, bounded by gentle sloping hills, which are covered with scrub oaks a few feet high, except where the land is in cultivation. Upon this cross road about three miles in length, equally accessible from Springfield by either of the roads we have mentioned, the rebel camp was situated.

Concealed by the shades of evening, on the 9th of August, General Lyon, with floating banners, but silent bands, emerged from the streets of Springfield, to attack by surprise, if possible, the foe, outnumbering him nearly three to one. His force was divided; one part under his own command, moved along the Mount Vernon road, to attack the enemy in front, while the other part, under the intrepid Colonel Sigel, with six pieces of artillery, two companies of cavalry, and several regiments of infantry, took the Fayetteville road, with instructions to attack the rebels in the rear. Precautions were taken, to render the surprise as complete as possible, and it was hoped that the rebels, distracted by the presence of an enemy, thus unexpectedly assailing them on both sides, and taken by surprise, might be effectually put to flight. It is proper to add, that the term of service of the Fifth Regiment of Missouri Volunteers, had expired; that Colonel Sigel, had gone to hem, company by company, and by his personal influence, had induced them to re-enlist for eight days; that this re-enlistment expired on the 9th, the day before the battle; that many of the officers had gone home, and that a considerable part of Sigel's force, was composed of raw recruits.

The morning of the 10th of August, was just beginning to dawn, when Colonel Sigel cautiously arrived within a mile of the rebel camp. So quietly did he advance, that some forty of the rebels going from their camp to get water and provisions, were taken prisoners without being able to give their commanders any warning of their danger. Silently the Union troops ascended the hills, which bordered the creek, and there beheld spread out before them, the tents of the foe. The rebels were at their breakfast. Colonel Sigel bringing his artillery into position, with a well directed shot into the midst of their encampment, gave the rebels the first intimation of his presence. They were thrown into utter disorder, by the suddenness of the surprise, and retreated in confusion down the valley. The infantry pursued, and quickly formed in the camp, so lately occupied by the rebels. The rebels, however, recovering from the first panic, were almost as quickly formed into line of battle, and Colonel Sigel found his little force opposed by one, three thousand strong. The artillerymen moved down into the valley, to co-operate with the infantry, and after a short fight, the enemy retired in some confusion. Meanwhile, the sound of heavy firing from the other end of the valley, was distinctly heard, and it was evident that Lyon was there, engaging the enemy in force. In order to aid Lyon, Colonel Sigel pressed forward his columns up the valley, selecting a position to cut off any attempted retreat of the enemy. He had already succeeded in taking over one hundred prisoners, when by a natural, but unfortunate mistake, his well-laid plans were overturned, and he was compelled to retreat. The firing in the north-west had ceased. He presumed that Lyon had been successful, and that his troops were in pursuit of the enemy. This was confirmed by the appearance to the east of him, of large bodies of rebels, apparently retreating to the south. Of course there could be no communications between him and Lyon, as the rebel force was directly between them. At this juncture, word was brought to Colonel Sigel, that Lyon's forces were advancing triumphantly up the road. His troops were told not to fire upon them, and with exultant hearts, they waved their flags, to those whom they supposed to be their victorious comrades.

Suddenly from the advancing troops, there burst upon Sigel's little band, a point-blank destructive fire, which covered the ground with the dying and the dead. At the same moment, from the adjoining hills, where they had supposed that Lyon's victorious troops were pursuing the enemy, there came plunging down upon them shot and shell, from a rebel battery. The Unionists were thrown into utter confusion, for they still believed that the volleys which swept their ranks, came from their friends. The gloom of the morning, and the absence of all uniform, prevented the prompt detection of the error. The cry ran from mouth to mouth, "our friends are firing upon us." The soldiers could not be dissuaded from this belief, until many had fallen. Nearly all the artillery horses were shot down at their guns, and death was sweeping the ranks. Most of these young patriots, had recently came from their peaceful homes, and had never before heard the spiteful whistle of a hostile bullet. It is not strange that a panic should have ensued. Under these circumstances, it might have been expected in the best drilled army. Five cannon were abandoned in the disorderly retreat. The foe, exultant and with hideous yells, came rushing on. Colonel Sigel himself, in his efforts to arrest the rout, narrowly escaped capture. With anguish, he afterwards summed up, that, out of his heroic little band, he had lost, in dead, wounded and missing, eight hundred and ninety-two. Some popular complaints have been uttered against Colonel Sigel, for not having afterwards, with the remnant of his forces, formed a junction with General Lyon. But this was not possible. There were but two roads, by which he could gain access to Lyon's position, at the other end of the valley. One was the long circuitous route of twenty miles, by the way of Springfield. The other, was the valley road, then in full possession of the exultant rebel army. There was, therefore, nothing for Colonel Sigel to do, but to withdraw his shattered and bleeding ranks as safely as possible, from the field.

General Lyon, meanwhile, having left Springfield at about the same time, with Colonel Sigel, arrived at one o'clock in the morning, in view of the enemy's camp-fires. Here his column lay, on its arms, till daylight, when it moved forward. The enemy had pickets thrown out at this point, and their surprise was therefore, less complete than it had been in the rear. By the time Lyon reached the northern end of the camp, he found the enemy prepared to receive him. He succeeded, however, after a brief struggle, in gaining a commanding eminence at the north of the valley, in which the camp was situated. Captain Plummer, with four companies of infantry, protected his left flank. The battle was now commenced, by a fire of shot and shell from Captain Totten's battery, and soon became general. In vain did the rebel host endeavor to drive Lyon from his well chosen position.

On the right, on the left, and in front, they assailed him, in charge succeeding charge, but in vain. His quick eye detected every movement, and successfully met and defeated it. The overwhelming number of the rebels, enabled them to replace, after each repulse, their defeated forces with fresh regiments, while Lyon's little band found no time for rest, no respite from the battle. The rebel host, surged wave after wave upon his heroic lines, as billows of the sea dash upon the coast. And as the rocks upon the coast beat back the flood, so did these heroic soldiers of freedom, with courage which would have ennobled veterans, and with patriotism which has won a nation's homage and love, hurl back the tireless surges of rebellion, which threatened to engulf them. It will be enough for any of these patriots to say. "I was at the battle of Wilson's Creek," to secure the warmest grasp of every patriot's hand.

Wherever the missiles of death flew thickest, and the peril of the battle was most imminent, there was General Lyon surely to be found. His young troops needed this encouragement on the part of their adored leader, and it inspired them with bravery, which nothing else could have conferred. His horse had been shot under him; three times he had been wounded, and, though faint from the loss of blood, he refused to retire even to have his wounds dressed; in vain did his officers beseech him to avoid so much exposure. It was one of those eventful hours, which Gen. Lyon fully comprehended, in which there was no hope but in despair. Again and again had the enemy been repulsed, only to return again and again with fresh troops, to the charge. Colonels Mitchell, Deitzler and Andrews, were all severely wounded. All the men were exhausted with the long and unintermitted battle, and it seemed as though one puff of war's fierce tempest would now sweep away the thin and tremulous line. Just then the rebels again formed in a fresh and solid column for the charge. With firm and rapid tread, and raising unearthly yells, they swept up the slope. General Lyon called for the troops standing nearest him to form for an opposing charge. Undaunted, and ready for the battle as ever, they inquired: "Who will be our leader?" "Come on, brave men," shouted Gen. Lyon, "I will lead you." In a moment he was at their head. At the next moment they were on the full run; at the next a deadly storm of bullets swept their ranks, staggering, but not checking them in their impetuous advance; on, on they rushed for God and liberty, and in another moment the foe were dispersed like dust by the gale. The victory was entire. This division of the rebels could rally no more. The army was saved; *but Lyon was dead!* Two bullets had pierced his bosom. As he fell, one of his officers sprang to his side, and inquired anxiously: "Are you hurt?" "Not much," was his faint reply. They were his last words. He fell asleep, to wake no more. O! hateful pro-slavery rebellion! Such are the victims immolated upon thy polluted shrine. Indignation is blended with the tears we shed over such sacrifices, which we have been compelled to offer to the demon of slavery. A nation mourned the loss of Lyon, the true Christian knight, without fear and without reproach. His remains now repose in the peaceful graveyard of his native village.

While passing this battle ground the soldiers picked up many human skulls and bones, which were scatted upon the earth, in the places, perhaps, where the soldiers to whom they belonged had fallen.

On Friday evening, (the 16th,) after twenty-four hours' retreat from Springfield, the rebel army was encamped on Crane Creek, twenty-nine miles distant. The Federal army was five miles in the rear, preparing to make an early start in pursuit next day. Price had placed his train in his advance. About one hundred wagons contained supplies, which were brought into Springfield from Forsyth only a few hours before the retreat was ordered. He will have some advantage among the hills, and the rebel sympathizers here claim that he will be reinforced by twelve or fifteen regiments from Bentonville, under General Van Dorn. On Friday afternoon four officers and thirteen privates were captured by our forces and sent to Springfield. They were captured near the rebel outposts by a squad of the First Missouri Cavalry. They were looking up mules, and got into our advance, supposing they were rebel pickets. The same evening Lieutenant Bushnell advanced on the rebel pickets with his mountain howitzer, and threw four shells, scattering them like sheep.

About six o'clock the army halted near Dug Springs, and prepared to bivouac for the night; but, before the preparations were completed, orders came to push forward. A messenger had announced that our cavalry was close upon the enemy, and desired that the infantry be sent forward in support. Hunger, fatigue, and all, were forgotten. Onward was the word, until twelve o'clock at night. The division of General Davis was in the advance, with the cavalry of Colonel Ellis and Major McConnel. The enemy had halted on Crane Creek, and, had not the night been so terribly dark, it is more than likely General Curtis would have attacked him immediately, but he was fearful of being drawn into an ambuscade. The troops lay on their arms awaiting the break of day.

At an early hour February 15th, the column moved forward, but during the night Price had again fled, leaving a large portion of his camp equipage, and a number of wagons. During that day the chase was very exciting, there being constant skirmishing between our advance and his rear guard. The road was strewn with broken wagons, dead and dying mules and horses, and every conceivable kind of goods. At four o'clock in the afternoon the booming of cannon notified us that Price had made a stand. The Dubuque battery was pushed forward, and for an hour we had a fine artillery fight. By the time our infantry got up the enemy had precipitately fled. On the 16th instant we pushed on, finding many evidences of the hasty flight in that day's march. During the afternoon our cavalry again overtook the rebels at Cross Timbers, and here was made a gallant charge by Colonel Harry Pease and forty men. Coming on the enemy's picket, they drove it in, dashing at once in the very midst of his camp. One of our men, a lieutenant of cavalry, was wounded, and five or six horses killed. The enemy's loss was much greater. The charge was really one of the most brilliant things that occurred on the route. On the 17th instant we had several skirmishes, and at last discovered the enemy in position on the south side of Sugar Creek. Taking it altogether the flight of Price, and our pursuit, will form one of the most interesting passages in the history of the war.

The valley through which Sugar Creek pursues its meandering course is nearly half a mile in width at Trott's Store. From the brows of the opposite ridges the distance is somewhat more, as the road winds. Skirmishing between the pickets of the two armies occurred during the morning, when Price moved out of sight beyond the brow of the south-western hills. His army, as was since ascertained, then formed in two lines on both sides of the road, and two Louisiana regiments, under command of Colonel Louis Herbert, which had arrived from Cross Hollows to reinforce Price, marched with their batteries, determined to give us a warm reception. Two of the enemy's cannon were planted on the brow of the hill, overlooking Sugar Creek, and their pieces were also ranged along the road, about two hundred yards apart, for half a mile or more. These pieces had prolongs attached, indicating that a running fight was intended in case of pursuit. In the meantime our cavalry formed on the opposite side of the valley, and marched across the creek to a point near Trott's Store, and halted. The enemy then opened fire from their batteries. One shot fell short, and a shell exploded over the heads of our men stationed on the opposite hill, doing no damage. Captain Hardin, of the Ninth Iowa Battery, answered the enemy's fire from the opposite bluff, throwing three shells from a howitzer with such good effect that the enemy were forced to fall back with their battery. General Curtis then ordered the cavalry to move up the hill and charge on the retreating foe. The order was gallantly obeyed by Colonel Ellis, in command of the First Missouri Cavalry, followed by Major Wright, leading his battalion, and Major McConnell, with the Third Battalion of the Third Illinois Cavalry. The whole force of our cavalry making the attack numbered some eight hundred. Gaining the brow of the hill, it was ascertained that they had fallen back over a mile to an open field, where their battery was again stationed, and the enemy in force, formed in line. Our cavalry, regardless of danger, plunged forward to the charge on the enemy's position, mostly screened by the intervening woods. Nothing could have withstood the impetuosity of such a charge, had not our advance, led by Colonel Ellis, when debouching from the woods into the open field, been met by a murderous fire poured in upon their ranks from behind the trees. Our loss was seven in killed and wounded at this point. Inevitable destruction, without a chance to resist so galling a fire, caused our brave men to recoil, when Colonel Ellis, with great coolness and presence of mind, ordered his men to right and left and scour the woods. The order was obeyed with telling effect on the enemy, many of whom were cut down behind their places of concealment, and the rest fled. Meantime Major McConnell, with his battalion, left the road, and, deploying to the left, advanced on the enemy's line, while Majors Wright and Boliver performed the same manouver on the right.

Two regiments of infantry arrived to support the cavalry, and formed in line. Colonel Phelps' regiment deployed on the left of the road, and Lieutenant-Colonel Herron, with the Ninth Iowa, deployed on the right. Captain Hayden, of the Dubuque battery, answered the enemy's batteries, which had opened upon our advancing columns, with a brisk fire. The cannonading was kept up for a few minutes, when the enemy precipitately fled, taking away most of his killed. Other regiments were coming into the field to take part in the ball. Among the latter was the Fourth Iowa. The men, anxious for the fray, had pulled off their coats and threw them aside.

There is little doubt that if the rebels had been followed up closely the route would have been complete, and no time would have been given them to burn their barracks at Cross Hollows.

The Colonel Herbert who commanded the rebel brigade was the gentleman of California notoriety, who slew the waiter at Willard's Hotel, a few years since. The other Confederate Colonels under him in the fight were McRae and McNair.

Among the badly wounded is J. A. Edwards, of Co. H, Eighth Indiana. He belonged to the infantry, but, getting possession of a horse, was the foremost in the fight, running the gauntlet of the leaden hail, which poured in upon him from the timber, without quailing. He got ahead of the cavalry, and was cut off by the enemy.

The Hospital Steward of the Third Illinois cavalry (Baker) had his horse shot down. He fell with the horse, dismounted, and leaped upon another horse in the melee, and rushed forward on the enemy with renewed vigor. Like Edwards, he had no business in the fight, but nothing could keep him from pushing to the front and have a "hand" in.

A man belonging to the Dubuque battery had his horse's head taken off by a cannon ball. He was leaning forward at the moment, and the ball passed just above him, doing no injury.

The inhabitants along this route, from Cassville to this point, were told by Price's army that the Northern troops were marching down, and were burning all the houses, ravishing the women, and killing the children. These ignorant people, it seems, believed the silly tale, and the result is that a general stampede took place. Men procured teams, gathered up what little valuables could be carried along, and, taking their families aboard, deserted their homes. Only three men were found in Cassville when our army arrived.

At Keetsville nearly all the inhabitants fled. From that point to Cross Hollows about two-thirds of the inhabitants on the road have deserted their dwellings. In several houses the tables were spread for breakfast, and in the hurry of flight were thus left. The wash-tub was seen filled with water on the back of the chair, indicating that the hegira occurred, as it actually did, on "wash-day." The doors were ajar, the clock on the mantelpiece had ceased ticking, feather beds were piled in the center of the floor, all sorts of furniture were scattered about, and not a sound was heard but the mewing of a cat. An air of lonesome, heart-sick desolation prevailed. One large dwelling was recently burned down, and the ruins were still smoking. Surely the leaders in this cursed civil war will have much to answer for.

Although strict orders forbid our boys from disturbing any private property, they, nevertheless, helped themselves to such things as they fancied. Clothing, quilts, dishes, cooking utensils, hams, lard, molasses, vinegar, meal, beans, and whatever else their hands inclined toward, was appropriated.

Rations at this time were very small, owing to having outmarched the provision train, and the boys were very glad to have such opportunities of filling up. Coffee had been played out several days before, and many had been restricted to hominy and parched corn. But now the fleeing rebels had left enough to more than satisfy their hunger, and they were not disposed to treat their liberality with contempt. Some Indiana troops threatened mutiny, on the 16th, in consequence of not having their proper provisions. They positively refused to march any farther until they were supplied with rations. Appropriations supplied them.

CHAPTER XII.

After laying in camp two days on Sugar Creek, resting from the wearisome march it had undergone since leaving Springfield, the regiment again moved out in the pursuit. After making somewhat of a circuitous rout by Osage Springs, it arrived in the neighborhood of Cross Hollows, and went into camp, on the 22d day of February—lacking three days of being one month since leaving Syracuse, Mo. During that time it had marched over two hundred and fifty miles.

Cross Hollows, from which Price's army has just disappeared beyond pursuit, is on the Fayetteville road. eighteen miles from that place, and sixteen miles from the Arkansas line, in Benton county. The road passes due south at this point, along the bed of a deep valley with precipitous sides, covered with brush, and the eminences covered with forests of black-jacks and swamp-oaks. Two other ravines cut across this valley at right angels, the other obliquely in a south-east and north-west direction. The junction of these ravines is called "Cross Hollows." A cantonment of three thousand Arkansas infantry has been located here during the winter. An excellent spring gushes forth under one of the banks, giving origin to a creek. It was thought that the six bold promontories, which send their salient points into the valley, would constitute natural ramparts for placing cannon to enfilade the

LIEUT. C.C. DOOLITTLE.

LIEUT. JOHN KELLY.

LIEUT. ANDERSON.

LIEUT. MOSSMAN.

LIEUT. R.D. IRVINE.

LIEUT. SANDERSON.

SERGT. T.J. MELVIN.

SERGT. CHS SMITH.

gorges and render the place impregnable, but it seems that the gorges were untenable in the face of the ardent troops of General Curtis. This is the last place at which it has been said by rebel sympathisers, that Price was going to give the Federal army battle. It is now said that he has fled to the mountains of Indian Territory, where it would be useless to undertake a pursuit.

Ben McCulloch arrived from Fort Smith the day before the fight at Sugar Creek, but did not participate in any part of the action, except the retreat. He insisted on making a stand at Cross Hollows, but Price objected. His habit of running has become a second nature to him. The stampede of the deluded people was exceeded only by the hurry of the rebel army to get away.

Camp Benjamin, located in a beautiful place, three miles west of Cross Hollows, in the principal valley, had one hundred and eight commodious huts erected, with chimneys in the center. The rebels burned all but five, and in the hurry of their flight, left thirty game cocks; some of these brandished silver spurs. Their best fighting material was thus evidently left behind. A book containing the general orders, and a quantity of brass knuckles were also left behind by the chivalry. It is a wonder to our troops why the two grist mills at this point were not fired.

As soon as the Federal army went into camp, many refugees returned to our lines, among whom were two intelligent women from their homes south of Fayetteville. They represented that their husbands were Union men, who fled to avoid being pressed into the rebel service. A threat was made that the wives of such who favored the Union cause would be hung, and many of these poor women were trying to make their way into

(6)

the Federal lines to escape this threatened doom. The day before these women left home, there were two Union men hung at Hewit's Mills. These women were piloted through to our lines by an intelligent contraband—the trusty slave of their father. This negro says that the retreat of Price was preceded by dispatches sent ahead, calling every citizen to arms. A perfect reign of terror prevails; committees were appointed to hang every man refusing to join the rebel army. People were removing their provisions to the woods and burying them, and fleeing in large numbers to the mountains. By a recent act, no negro must be found beyond his master's premises, under pain of thirty-nine lashes, administered on the bare back. A few weeks since, five negroes caught fishing together in a stream, twelve miles from Fayetteville, were hung, and their bird-pecked carcass can be seen swinging in the air to this day, as a warning to others. The negros are told that the Northern Abolitionists are trying to get them in their power for the purpose of transporting them to Cuba. This negro says that the war has made the Southern men "mighty temperate;" none but the vilest corn whisky can be procured. The "quality" are suffering headaches from being deprived of their accustomed beverage, coffee. Sassafras tea, used as a substitute, sweetened with sorghum, was not generally relished. Coffee in Fayetteville held at sixty cents a pound, and none could be had even at that price. Sheeting and shirting was worth one dollar a yard. The negro made a statement to General Curtis, and gave the latter a plan showing the roads through the Boston Mountains. Full confidence is placed in his statement. The two women and negro were sent forward to Springfield.

On the evening of the 24th, the head of a train on

the way, five miles this side of Keitsville, and four wagons belonging to a Sutler of the Twenty-Second Indiana, were burned. The balance of the train, containing five days provisions, was several miles behind, and returned to Cassville. On the same evening, Captain Montgomery's command, of Wright's battalion, stationed at Keitsville, was attacked by eight hundred and fifty Texan Rangers, under Colonel Young. Montgomery and his men escaped to Cassville, with the loss of two killed, one wounded and one taken prisoner. Seventy-five horses were left in possession of the rebels. The enemy, it appears, came on our pickets in the dark. In reply to "who comes there?" the answer was, "a friend." The rebels then rushed forward, the pickets fired, but were overpowered. The enemy rushed into Keitsville and fired upon the house occupied by the cavalry. Captain Montgomery did not order a fire in the darkness and confusion, as his men and the enemy became undistinguishable. The rebels had two killed and one wounded. They said they were Texan Rangers, encamped on Sugar Creek, and had burned one of our trains and intended to destroy another.

On the 21st, one of the First Missouri Cavalry ventured into Bentonville, the county seat of Benton county, five miles from Cross Hollows, alone; got into difficulty with some citizens, and was literally stoned to death. The next day, the company to which he belonged retaliated by burning several houses and razing the town generally.

While laying here, the news came to camp, that the Ninth Regiment of Missouri Volunteers was no longer a Missouri regiment, but was now numbered among the honored regiments of its own State, and was hereafter to be known as the Fifty-Ninth Illinois Regiment. The news was received with acclamations of hearty satisfaction. Colonel Julius White, who now commanded the brigade, read the dispatch announcing the fact, and the Major of the regiment, P. Sidney Post, made some few, well chosen and congratulatory remarks, which were received with three hearty cheers. Three cheers for Colonel White; three for Colonel C. H. Frederick, and three times three for the State of Illinois.

While at the Lamoine, some time in January, Captain S. W. Kelly, Captain Winters and Captain Elliott got up a petition to the Secretary of War, to have the regiment transferred from the Missouri to the Illinois service. Nine-tenths of the men in the regiment were from that State, and the feeling was almost universal in favor of the transfer. In order to add weight and influence to the petition, they procured the signatures of General Palmer and Colonel White, now commanding brigade, and, with one exception, all the line officers of the regiment. Colonel Frederick being a citizen of Missouri, and having used great exertions and made much personal sacrifice to recruit and organize the regiment for his own State, did not feel inclined to encourage the petition. Yet he most generously withheld any effort to prevent its free circulation and passage to the Secretary of War; and after the transfer, he withheld not his kindly feeling towards the regiment, nor spared any labor to promote its efficiency or welfare. Through the personal influence of General Palmer, the Adjutant General of Illinois, and Governor Yates became interested in the matter, and through *their* exertions the petition was acted upon.

CHAPTER XIII.

On the 24th, the regiment moved to a more pleasant situation, and anticipated going into regular camp for some time, as it was rumored that the campaign was now fully lengthened out, and that the tents and extra baggage that had been left at Lebanon was coming up. The army also needed rest. The grounds were accordingly measured off in military style, and tents pitched in systematic order. The weather is delightful, and if the men had plenty of rations, they would enjoy it hugely; but hunger is annoying. There was a scarcity of provisions, and for several days coffee had disappeared from camp. It was two hundred miles to our base of supplies, and mule teams are proverbially slow, especially in muddy roads and with lazy drivers. The country is scouted over by the boys, but they find little to compensate them for their trouble. The citizens have nothing left for themselves.

Colonel Kelton was recalled to St. Louis, soon after returning from Springfield, in the fall, and placed on the staff of General Halleck. Major McGibbon had also returned to St. Louis, and in consequence, their positions were vacant in the regiment. Camp Halleck, where the regiment now lay, was the first since leaving the Lamoine, that afforded any leisure for consultations as to who should fill these important positions. The result of several night meetings of the officers of the regiment, was the election of P. Sidney Post to the position of Colonel, and Captain J. C. Winters to that of Major.

P. Sidney Post left a promising law practice in Galesburg, Ill., and came to St. Louis with Captain Clayton Hale's company, (company A,) and at the organization of the regiment received the appointment of Adjutant. This position he had filled with entire satisfaction to the regiment and credit to himself. And from this position had, deservedly, been promoted to the position of Major, and from Major *now* to the Colonelcy.

Lieut. Colonel C. H. Frederick had commanded the regiment ever since leaving Boonville, to the entire satisfaction of the men in the ranks; but being a strict disciplinarian, both as regarded men and officers, he had procured the ill will of some of the latter, and hence the election of the regimental Major to the position which rightfully belonged to him. Such injustice frequently occurs in the army.

Captain J. C. Winters commanded a company, (G,) which he had recruited near White Hall, Ill., and was richly deserving the position of Major. He had served in the Mexican war, and was one of the first military men in the regiment.

The regiment now lay basking in the sun shine for several days. Their time was spent in discussing rumors concerning the enemy, and in taking a retrospect of their previous hardships and long marches.

The rumors to be discussed were that Price was now at Boston Mountains filling up and preparing his army for a return to give us battle, and drive the invaders from Arkansas and Missouri. The retrospect included the time spent in marches since leaving St. Louis up to the present at Camp Halleck.

It was now only five months since leaving the arsenal at St. Louis, and the regiment had marched over seven hundred miles. Camp Halleck is six miles south of Bentonville, the county town of Benton county. Benton county is the north-west county of Arkansas. To get here, the regiment left Boonville, Mo., and marched to Syracuse; from thence to Otterville; thence to Sedalia, Warsaw, Bolivar, and Springfield. Then from Springfield through Warsaw back to Syracuse. Then from Syracuse to Sedalia and back to Otterville. From Otterville to Typton, thence by Lynn Creek Ferry across the Osage to Lebanon and on to Springfield. From Springfield through Cassville, Keitsville and Bentonville to Camp Halleck, Arkansas.

Another matter of discussion is, "where to, next?" This is not known, but one thing is known, and that is, that a march of two or three hundred miles is before us. We are two hundred miles west of Cairo, three hundred or more from St. Louis, and these are the two points nearest home. If we go on south, it is eighty miles to the nearest steam boat landing, on the Arkansas River, and there is no probability of *our* riding on a steam boat, so that to do the very best we can, we have two hundred miles to march.

And still another topic of conversation, is the probabilities of a speedy termination of the war. Those who have been home on furloughs, and are now returning, bring reports that the people at home and around St. Louis, are firmly in the belief that peace will soon be proclaimed. The soldier's heart expands with joy at these glad tidings. If all the armies of the Union have been as successful as *this*, the joy and hope is not delusive. May the hope of a speedy termination of the war be not as delusive as the anticipation that the Fifty-Ninth would have a long rest in Camp Halleck.

On the morning of the 1st of March, General Davis' division broke up camp near Osage Springs, and fell back about ten miles, to a stronger position on Sugar Creek. The Fifty-Ninth Illinois Regiment going into camp on the summit of one of the small mountains of this region. This is not really a mountainous country, yet the hills are so gigantic that *mountain* would not be an improper appellation. The hill on which the Fifty-Ninth is encamped is three hundred feet above the bed of Sugar Creek, in the valley below, and seems to be composed of millions of little rocks thrown together in one huge pile. Its surface is literally nothing else but fractional pieces of stone—and these the soldier must have for his bed. Yet he sleeps soundly.

The second day of March came in cold, and during the day some snow fell, as did also on the 3d and 4th. This made it very disagreeable in camp. Short rations, thin clothing, and some with bare feet, caused a good deal of suffering and no little discontent among the troops.

An incident, new and intensely interesting, occurred to the Fifty-Ninth on the afternoon of the 5th of March. Sometime in January, a slight difficulty had occurred between Captain ―――― and one of his men, in relation to who should furnish the Captain's fire with wood. The Captain was inclined to have his fire supplied with wood at the expense of the dignity of this young private, and the young man was determined he should not, and hence came the charge of "disobedience of orders." Before, however, the thing was entirely settled some further difficulties occurred, and the young man was threatened with corporeal punishment;

this he resisted with his knife, cutting the clothes of the Lieutenant of the company, and threatening to take his life. This added to the previous charge, one of still greater gravity. The young man was court-martialed, and sentenced to have his head shaved, his uniform taken from him, and to be drummed out of the service.

On the afternoon of the 5th, this farce was played off, to the delight of some, and the disgust of many. The whole division was called out and formed in two lines across an open field in the valley, to witness the great show. At an appointed time, the young man made his appearance at one end of the amphitheater, with shaved head, uncovered, accompanied by two guards with fixed bayonets, and a fife and drum following in his rear. To the tune of the rogues march, he was thus paraded from one end of the line to the other, and back to the place of beginning. The farce was now over, and the young man supposed to be forever ruined. But not so. It only made him a hero and martyr in the eyes of the soldiers. Their sympathies were all excited in his favor. They saw in the act nothing but tyranny, on the part of the officers who pronounced the sentence, and folly in its execution.

On returning to camp, a subscription was raised in his behalf, and quite a sum was donated to defray his expenses to parts unknown. He went to Cassville, and immediately enlisted in the Montgomery Guards, and about the time his hair had grown to a respectable length, he married one of the fairest maidens of the country.

Rumors now began to thicken, that the enemy was really returning upon us. And in fact they were, for on the morning of the 6th, they made an attack upon

General Sigel, at Bentonville, and drove him to the main lines at Sugar Creek.

General Curtis, in anticipation of an attack, had erected some fortifications in and around the main crossing of Sugar Creek—which he prided himself very much with, but which, in fact, were small affairs. After General Sigel had safely placed his command in position, he reported to General Curtis in person. The General received him at the door, and before asking him in, inquired his opinion in regard to the fortifications he had erected. General Sigel merely glanced his eyes over the works, and without any remarks, inquired if General Curtis had anything to eat at his quarters, as he was almost starved to death, and alighting from his horse, walked into the tent without a word of the fortifications. He seemed to think that his supper was of more importance than General Curtis' fortifications.

CHAPTER XIV.

The morning of the 7th of March broke clear and pleasant over the hills and valley of Sugar Creek and Cross Timbers. The soldiers were everywhere, early on the alert, and camp presented a good deal the appearance of a bee-hive on a sunny morning. Better spirits than had been for several days seemed to prevail among the boys, and all was cheerful. There seemed to be no thought that before another morning should break on Cross Timbers, many who now felt so buoyant and full of hope would be numbered among the "brave boys slain." Little did they realize that this bright morning was the harbinger of such a bloody sun-set as closed this day, over the battle-ground of Pea Ridge.

About seven o'clock orders were received at regimental head-quarters to strike tents immediately, and move out toward the right. The right, or, rather, rear of the army, lay at this time across the road leading to Cassville. The regiment, as soon as the tents and camp equipage could be loaded in the wagons, moved in a circuitous route, through the brush, until it struck the Cassville road, one mile north of Sugar Creek. Here it filed to the right, and halted, about fifty yards east of the road, apparently to wait further orders. It seemed as though the plan of the battle was yet undecided. An hour elapsed while in this position, and then the order came to "fall in." The regiment now retraced its steps to the road, and again stacked arms. In a short time thereafter, several horsemen were seen coming down the road from the right, at break-neck speed. Some had lost their hats, some their coats, some their guns, and nearly all of them had lost their wits. "The rebels—the rebels are coming in the rear!" was their war cry, as they charged along the road toward some place of safety. They received, and deserved, the jeers of the soldiers, as they passed.

The rebels had made a slight attack on the rear as a feint, and these cowardly cavalry had fled to save their paltry carcasses from the rebel balls. Shame on such dastards!

It was now eleven o'clock, and the enemy was attacking our left wing in earnest. Davis' division now moved forward on the double-quick, through Leetown, and half a mile beyond, where it formed in line as rapidly and judiciously as the brushy condition of the position would admit. On the road leading west from Leetown, and three-quarters of a mile distant, is an open field of, perhaps, twenty acres, with a cross fence through its center, and skirted with densely thick underbrush all around it. On the east side of this field the Fifty-Ninth and Thirty-Seventh Illinois were placed in line. When first gaining this position, no enemy were in sight, but very soon a column of men were seen filing through the timber, to the left of the field, and coming into line in our front. At first it was supposed to be a column of our own men, as the thickness of the underbrush prevented from distinguishing the motly uniforms of the rebels from our own. The mistake was soon discovered by some of the men, but the order to fire was withheld from our boys until a volley from the rebel column was poured into them. Then the fact that it was the enemy became too evident, and the fire was returned with double interest. The firing now became incessant. Volley after volley, in quick succession, was sent by our brave boys into the falling ranks of the enemy. For a long time it seemed as though no impression was being made upon the column of the enemy, although those who were not engaged could see men falling from their ranks by scores. They kept their ranks always full, by marching fresh regiments up to take the place of decimated ones. Thus one single, unrelieved line, stood and fought five different regiments, from one o'clock until darkness closed the scene. The first fire from the enemy killed and wounded several of the men of both regiments, but it created no panic, no confusion, in either. The Fifty-Ninth only replied with a more hearty good will. At one time their ammunition gave out, and they fell back to a safer position, until it could be replenished. They then advanced to their old position, and let into the rebels with increased energy.

During the whole afternoon not a man flinched, not an officer wavered. One or two subordinate officers failed to share the honors of the battle, by being dilatory about going in, and a very few of the men; but those that were there did their whole duty, and more than prudence demanded of them.

Companies K and F suffered more in killed and wounded than any other two companies, from their being in a more exposed position, on the left of the regiment. At the first fire several of their men fell. Captain Snyder, commanding Company K, and Captain Kelly, commanding Company F, by their coolness and good judgment, soon manouvered their companies into such positions as was most destructive against the enemy, and most protective to themselves. During the whole action these two officers displayed a bravery and clearness of judgment worthy of all imitation. Captains Hale, Paine, Winters, Elliott, Veatch and Taylor, alike deserve honorable mention for their bravery and daring during the engagement. Each vied with the other in proper conduct and exemplary bravery. Colonel Frederick and Major Post were ever present where duty called, fearless of consequences. Although constantly exposed, Colonel Frederick escaped unharmed; not so with Major Post. About the middle of the afternoon, a minnie ball struck him on the arm, passing through the fleshy parts without injury to the bone, and yet making a severe wound. He retired to have his arm dressed, and then, only by the peremptory order of the Surgeon, was he prevented from going back into the fight.

The Assistant Surgeon of the regiment, Doctor H. J. Maynard, now acting Surgeon, in the absence of Doctor Hazlett, established his head-quarters at Leetown, where the wounded were ordered to be brought for surgical attention. Very soon after the first volley the wounded began to arrive, and continued to come, as fast, and sometimes faster, than they could be attended to, the remainder of the day. Thirty-eight from the Fifty-Ninth alone were brought in. Doctor Maynard, assisted by his Hospital Steward, (the writer of these pages,) by his surgical skill and kindness of treatment, made these men as comfortable as the nature of their wounds would admit.

The names of those brought from the field wounded are as follows:

From Company K: James Yocum, Corporal Willard W. Sheppard, Corporal William Burns, John B. Bass,

V. S. Hawk, Julius Hiederick, Emuel Herbert, James Higgins, Sergeant Peter Elliott, Patrick Powers, John J. Rue, and James Donathy, wounded. Michael D. Sullivan, of this company, was killed on the field. Thirteen wounded, and one killed.

The wounded of Company F were: John W. Williams, Silas P. Kamer, Sergeant Samuel J. Spohn, Hiram Snearly, John Chittenden, William Welker, David Groves, and Davis L. Kelly. James H. Furgueson, of Company F, was killed on the field. Eight wounded, and one killed.

Company B had two wounded, viz: Richard Ernest, and G. B. Finch, and one killed on the field—G. W. Evans.

The wounded of Company H were: William H. Smith, John L. Ransom, William N. McGowan, John W. Hurst. Peter P. Goodman was killed on the field. Four wounded, and one killed.

Company D lost three killed on the field, to wit: Eugene Cramball, Henry Spohn, and Isaac Palmer.

Company I lost three killed—Alfred B. Blake, Henry Cramer, and William H. Cline.

Company C, one wounded—James Murphy.

There were a few whose names the writer has mislaid and forgotten.

Toward evening the fire began to slacken, and by five o'clock had entirely ceased, both armies being willing to withdraw from the contest. The Fifty-Ninth fell back to the east of Leetown, a short distance, and lay on their arms till morning.

On the morning of the 8th, just as the sun began to redden the eastern horizon, the booming of cannon was heard from the direction of Cassville. It was very soon ascertained that General Sigel had engaged with the enemy, on our right. The Fifty-Ninth was soon in motion toward the scene of action. Arriving on the ground, they were placed in position, again in front of the enemy, and similar to yesterday, with an open field between them. They remained in this position but a short time, when they were ordered to charge across the field, and rout the enemy from the woods beyond. This was accomplished without the loss of a man. The enemy were driven from the woods, and the Fifty-Ninth had played its part of this great tragedy. Their position, before making the charge, was behind a fence, in range of a rebel battery, and the shot from this battery was very annoying, although no one was hit by it. They lay on their stomachs, so that the shot, for the most part, passed over them. Occasionally one would fall short, and throw the dirt into their faces, through the cracks in the fence. One, in particular, struck so near to the head of one of the boys as to fill his eyes completely. "D—n the thing," said he, and, twisting himself around, until his other end was directed toward the enemy, he remarked that "now they might shoot, and be d—d." While making the charge, a musket-ball passed through the clothing of Captain Kelly, and dropped into his boot-leg. In the early part of the day, while Colonel Frederick was riding in front of the regiment, a twelve-pound cannon-ball passed so close to his head as to knock him from his horse, insensible. It was several hours before he could be restored to consciousness, and many days before he entirely recovered from the concussion.

During the fight of the 7th, very many narrow escapes of the men occurred. One boy, while loading his gun, had the ram-rod knocked from his hand, by a musket ball from the enemy. Another one had his gun-barrel hit, and bent so bad as to be useless. One man had three bullets to pass through his hat, and many escaped with holes through different parts of their clothing. The great wonder is, that all were not killed—their escape can only be accounted for, on the principles that "God and right was on our side."

An anecdote was told of the regimental hospital nurse, who is a "live Dutchman in a fight," and when not employed, was always in the front. Soon after the engagement commenced, he, with his gun, was standing near Davidson's battery, looking at the scene, when one of the battery-men discovered a rebel, in the distance, making preparations to shoot at him. The battery-man warned him of his danger, and pointed to the rebel; instantly the nurse raised his gun, and both guns cracked at the same time. The rebel fell, and Ebling was unharmed.

During the night of the 7th, Dr. Maynard, had a sufficient number of tents pitched, to shelter comfortably all the wounded, and the morning of the 8th presented a sad, but lively appearance at Leetown. Cooks and nurses, were active in providing for and administering to the wants of the unfortunate heroes of the day before. Nothing that would tend to alleviate their sufferings, was neglected. Long will the wounded of Pea Ridge, remember Dr. H. J. Maynard.

Sunday, the 9th, was a day of rest to the Fifty-Ninth. The enemy had disappeared, and all was quiet over the hills of Cross Timbers. The soldiers had nothing to do, but wander over the battle-field, and talk of the incidents of the two day's fight. And this was enough for one day. The dead and wounded were, many of them, still on the field. The rebel dead were all unburied, and many of their wounded were uncared for.

(7)

Detachments from the rebel army were busy, under a flag of truce, in collecting and carrying their wounded to hospital, and in burying their dead. Many are hid away in the bushes, who will never have a burial. Years hence, their bones will be discovered bleaching in the sun. Such is the case on every battle field. Friend and foe alike, are left undiscovered. Some, perhaps, mortally wounded, crawl away to the shelter of a friendly thicket, that they may escape capture by the enemy, and here remain, until death claims them for his own. Months hence, they are discovered, and then the cry goes out, that the enemy is barbarous, because the dead were left unburied.

The scene over this field of carnage, beggars all description. Sights calculated to chill the blood, and strike the mind with horror, meet you on every side. Here is a human body, with the mangled remnants of a head, which a cannon ball has torn to fragments. There lies another with both legs shot away. Here is one, the top of whose skull is gone, leaving the brain all exposed to the weather, and see! he is still alive. After twenty-four hours in this condition, he yet lives. Great is the tenacity of human life! Look yonder! there is one whose light of life has gone out, as a lighted lamp in a gentle wind. There is no disturbance of features, no marks of violence about him. He is sitting at the roots of a large tree, with his back supported by the trunk; his gun is resting in the bend of his arm; how natural! while sitting thus, a minnie ball had pierced his heart, and thus he died. The number on his cap denotes the regiment to which he belongs, which is now in another part of the field; thus accounting for his not having yet received burial. Ah! here comes two men with the same numbers on their caps that he has on his, and they are in search of him. How fortunate they are. They are his friends and were his messmates. How sad to find him thus, what news to send his friends at home! His mother! 'Twill break her heart; so loved was he, so loved by all who knew him. He had a premonition of his doom the morning of the battle, and told his friends so, told them he would be killed that day, and gave them all his letters and his pictures of the dear ones at home. Among them was a picture of his hearts beloved, his betrothed, an angel in beauty. These two friends weep, and we pass on.

What is that fellow doing? That fellow in the dress of a Union soldier, what is he doing? He is rifling the pockets of the dead. Let's see what he has found in that man's pocket. A small pocket book, and a letter or two, pen knife and comb. The pocket book has two or three dollars of confederate script, for the dead man was a rebel, and a locket of hair, very fine silky hair, evidently clipped from the locks of some very young person, perhaps an infant daughter. How mean this Union soldier is, to rob the parent dead of this cherished memento of his lovely little daughter! Why not bury it with him?

The man those men are lifting so carefully into the ambulance yonder, was wounded yesterday morning, and has been lying on the cold ground without any covering, ever since. His wound was not a mortal one, but now his limbs are all stiffened by the exposure, and his life is the sacrifice. Had he remained a short time longer in his exposed condition, he would have added one more to the number of these they are collecting for burial, over in that pleasant grove. The grave is being dug, and only seven have yet been found to fill it. It is large enough to hold at least a dozen. The Union soldier, when buried by his comrades, is generally buried in a civilized manner; but rebels are traitors together, while living, and are not separated in the grave, when dead. Such are a few of the many interesting sights that meet the eye, in passing over the battle ground of Pea Ridge, on this Sabbath morning.

Sergeant Silas Carner, and private John Williams, of Company F, died in the hospital from the effects of their wounds on the 8th, and were buried with the honors of war. Wm. N. McGowan, of Company H, Samuel J. Spohwn of Company F, and John W. Hurst of Company H, died, the two former on the 12th, and the latter on the 13th. Wm. N. McGowan was one of the musicians for the regiment. It was his duty to beat the drum, not to handle the musket; but when he saw his comrades marching to the battle, his brave heart spurned the idea of his remaining idle. He shouldered a musket, fell into ranks with his old company, and manfully assisted in repelling the foe. He remained on the field doing his duty, until towards the close of the day's battle, when a minnie ball struck him, and he was brought off mortally wounded. He lingered, under great suffering, but with a proud consciousness of the noble sacrifice he was making for his country, until the morning of the 12th, when he expired with the resignation of a hero. All honor to the brave! In this brave boy's pocket, was twenty dollars in money, which was placed in the hands of Captain ——, to be forwarded to his widowed mother, at Charleston, Illinois. Several months afterwards, the writer was informed, by letter received from this poor widow woman, that the money had never been given to her. Captain —— resigned his commission soon after the battle of Pea Ridge, and it is to be hoped he found a resting place in some parts *unknown* to anybody. Many a dollar, belonging to the dead soldier, has been thus appropriated.

After a very stormy night, Monday morning came in clear and pleasant, and hundreds of idle soldiers were scattered over the battle field, to the west of Leetown, in search of whatsoever might be found there. General Davis' Division was lying to the east, and General Sigel's to the north of town. About eight o'clock, boom went a cannon, from the direction of Sigel's camp, and a shell went hurling over Leetown, in the direction of the battle field. Soon another followed, and at the same time a column of cavalry was seen approaching from the west, which was supposed to be rebel. "The rebels are coming, the rebels are coming," was shouted from mouth to mouth, over the field, and each one broke for his regiment. The attention of all in town, was attracted by the reports of the guns, and the street was soon lined by the curious, eager to know what was up. "The rebels are coming," came up the street, followed closely by scores of fleeing soldiers, some on horseback, but many more on foot, each vieing with the other, as to who should get out of the way the quickest. "The rebels are coming, stop them!" cries a horseman, with hat off and hair flying in the wind. "What's up?" asks one of the boys of this valorous horseman. "The rebels are coming, and I am trying to stop these fellows—halt there!" and away he goes, more frightened than the rest. Pretty soon, General Sigel comes riding very deliberately up the road, by himself, and some one asks him the cause of the stampede. "Oh, nothing," said he, with a peculiar twinkle of the eye, "I was only making a few of my leetle arrangements." Discipline had become too loose to suit his military fancy, and he had arranged this scare for the purpose of putting the army on the *quie vive*. In five minutes after the first report, the whole army was under arms, ready for any emergency. The first shell fired, struck not far from a forage train that was bringing in corn, and the way they came into camp was a caution to all mule drivers. No one was hurt, only in feelings.

CHAPTER XV.

On the afternoon of the 10th, the regiment moved with the division, a few miles south of Leetown, and here the writer lost sight of it for several days, as he was detained at the hospital to assist in caring for the wounded. Nothing, however, of interest occurred during his absence, except the visit of the Paymaster, and a few changes of camp.

By remaining at hospital, the writer escaped much hard fare, as the army was, for several days, entirely destitute of provisions, and subsisted solely on parched corn and *nothing else.* By very great exertions, Dr. Maynard succeeded in keeping a supply at the hospital, until the orders came to move all the wounded to Cassville, twenty miles farther north.

On the 14th, the wounded were started for Cassville; some were too badly hurt to be handled so roughly, and were not sent. Among these were James Murphy and John L. Ransom, and John B. Bass, who had a leg amputated. James Murphy died on the 18th. The others were subsequently brought up. The writer was ordered to report at Cassville with the wounded, and here is an extract from a letter written to his daughter soon after his arrival:

"Wednesday morning, the 19th. I am up pretty early this morning as usual. The sun is just beginning to tinge the horizon with his red beams, and the promise of a pretty day is written on the sky above him. The night has been a stormy one. It was raining when I spread my blankets, but now the sky is clear, the atmosphere pure and bracing, and indicates a few days of fine spring weather. Spring is opening earlier here than in Illinois, as we are farther south. If you will examine, you will find that Cassville is more than two hundred miles south of where you live, and of course the climate is more mild and the seasons earlier. We have had quite a number of warm, spring-like days, and the grass looks quite green. The buds on the trees will soon open out, and it will not be long till nature will all be clothed in its summer garb.

"Cassville is situated in a pretty location. It is in a small valley, surrounded by hills of different magnitude. On the east are several ridges of considerable highth, dotted on their sides with cedar trees in green, which are nature to the rocky hill sides of this region. At the foot of one of these ridges, a four story mill contrasts her white coating of paint with the green of the cedar, and produces a pleasing, romantic picture. A small stream meanders along at the base of those hills, with here and there a spring gushing from among the rocks, or boiling up from even the bed of the stream. On the west there are also hills of considerable highth. The valley is a mile wide, and two or three miles long, or perhaps more. The soil is rich and productive. From my room I can look out over a field of wheat, which completely clothes the ground in living green. It is quite refreshing to sit here, and look upon a green spot of earth, after having contemplated only the sear and barren trunks of trees and brush for four long months of winter. From another window I can see a pretty little cottage, white as the driven snow, nestled in among the surroundings of a cultivated home. A large fine orchard, and all the out-buildings of comfort, and all deserted. Wounded soldiers are spread over the floors of the house, and soldiers' horses are tied to and destroying the fruit trees, and soldiers' fires have burned the rails and boards which inclose the premises. Dreadful are the ravages of war! Cassville is situated in the center of this valley, and was a thriving, pretty town before the war. There are about forty good dwelling houses, six store rooms, and a very decent little court house, besides blacksmith shops, &c.

"When we came here, there were only four families remaining in town, and they were women and children, the men being in the army. Now, there are over four hundred wounded and sick soldiers quartered here; every house is full and some are in tents outside. The houses are being torn up, so as to be made more convenient for bedding the wounded. The fencing before the door yard is being torn down and burned, and anything which adds to the comfort and convenience of those here, is being appropriated without let or hindrance.

There is another pretty town, five miles from here, in precisely the same condition, filled with sick and wounded. These two towns are samples of all the towns in Missouri, where the armies have been. The citizens have fled and the soldiers have destroyed their property. Many fine houses have been burned on our march, and others entirely riddled, windows broken, doors torn from their hinges, &c. Both armies are engaged in destroying; what the enemy leaves, our men destroy. The enemy destroys Union property, and the Union troops destroy secesh property—and there being only the two kinds of property, it is ALL destroyed.

"An express rider has just came in from the army, bringing news that Price is moving towards them again. We, here, can't tell what reliance can be given the report. If it is true, and he should continue to advance, there will be some more hard fighting. I do most sincerely hope that our regiment may not get into another engagement here. If it should, we, in the hospital, will not get away from here for two or three months to come, unless Price should be victorious and drive us out on double quick; for the wounded will be brought here, and of course will prolong our time as much longer as the difference between the time of the first fight and that which shall come off now. But it is not on account of that alone, that I am unfriendly to another battle. I have seen enough of the suffering attending the wounded of the last battle. Poor fellows! They bear it patiently, and make light of the most serious wounds. I do not suppose it would be very interesting to you to read a description of the wounds we have to dress every morning, or I would describe some of them. We have eighty different wounds to dress in our building, and you can imagine how great the variety. Some are about the head, some about the body, arms, legs, feet and hands; some are only slightly wounded, but the majority are badly hurt. One poor fellow died yesterday, from the effect of a ball through the lungs; and others will die from their wounds. Our men are well provided for here. They have all the attention from Surgeons and nurses that they require, and all the food and other comforts necessary for them. Dr. Clark, of the Thirty-Seventh Illinois Volunteers, is our Surgeon. Dr. Maynard was left with the regiment. I am in charge of the wounded from our regiment, and Thomas Kelly is with us as Warden. We two are the only ones of our acquaintances here, excepting Hiram Snearly, who is quite badly wounded, the ball passing through the arm, close to the shoulder, and into the side under the arm, and coming out below the shoulder blade behind. His wound seems to be doing well, yet it is difficult to tell what the result may be. I shall now retire from the desk, and finish this short epistle at some other sitting.

"I am sleepy to-day, at three o'clock, because of not sleeping well last night. The floor, some how or other, was unusually hard last night, and caused me to be restless. I prophesied fair weather yesterday—this is the 20th—but was deceived by appearances. We are very often deceived by appearances. In an hour after I had made the prophesy, the sky was completely clouded over, and has remained so ever since; and now it is spitting snow.

"Reports are still coming in of the advance of the enemy, and the retreat of our army. It is said that Price has been strongly reinforced, and now numbers more men than he did at first. We have also been reinforced to the number of one thousand men, but are still far inferior, as to number, to the enemy. It is probable, that our army will make a stand at or near Keitsville, eight miles from here, where, if the enemy comes upon them, they will have a hard fight.

"The Fifty-Ninth and the Thirty-Seventh Illinois regiments, occupied the court house as an hospital. Dr. Clark, of the Thirty-Seventh Illinois, having the supervision of the whole.

"On the 23d of March, it became evident that Johnson Kelly, of company D, Fifty-Ninth Regiment Illinois Volunteers, would either have to undergo the operation of having his leg amputated, or lose his life—

or perhaps both. Dr. Clark proceeded to the operation. Chloroform was administered in the usual manner, and the leg taken off without the knowledge of the patient. The amputation was very handsomely performed, but it proved to be useless. In four hours the patient was dead. Johnson Kelly was buried with the honors of war, on the 24th of March, 1862. Hiram Snearly lingered until the 22d of April, 1862, with the hope firmly fixed in his mind that he would get well. He was told by the Surgeon and by his friends, that he could not survive, but he believed them not. His spirits were buoyant to the very last hour of his existence. He died and was also buried with the honors of a soldier.

"A day or two after coming to Cassville, Dr. Clark requested a detail from the Provost Marshall, to clean up around the court house. Captain Montgomery happened to have a squad of rebel prisoners at Cassville, at this time, and they were set to work picking up the rubbish in the court house yard—Captain Montgomery overseeing them himself. From the wrongs his family had received at their hands, his heart had become entirely callous to any pity. With the greatest apparent satisfaction, he rode round among these fellows very much like one of their own negro drivers, with whip in hand and bitter curses on his tongue; and if one ceased from his labor, whack went the whip and glib the tongue.

"Among these prisoners was an intelligent Catholic priest, from Louisiana. This morning he was unwell, and entirely unaccustomed to picking up chips, his progress at work was rather slow. The Captain seemed to take special delight in tormenting him. 'Well,' says he, 'old fellow I pity you, indeed; but it can't be helped

You must take care in the future to be caught in better company. If you had kept out of the company of these imps of hell, you would not now be degrading yourself by manual labor—work away then my old priesty.'"

CHAPTER XVI.

On the 6th of April the Fifty-Ninth, with the balance of the Division, arrived at Cassville, en route for Forsyth, which is sixty miles east of here. After halting long enough to rest, and visit their wounded friends in hospital, they moved out some two miles to the east of the town, and encamped on Big Mill Creek. The march was continued on the seventh, through the most dreary and least inhabited portion of Missouri that the army had yet seen. For seven or eight miles east of Cassville the soil is arid, and covered with small white flint-stone, with here and there a miserably poor specimen of a black-jack, struggling for a scanty existence. From this upper plateau of the Ozark Mountains, the road drops down through a narrow defile, with hills two hundred feet high on either side, the base of the hills meeting so close at the foot as barely to admit the passage of a wagon, until it emerges into the Rock House Creek Valley. From this point the valley begins to widen to the south, where, as far as the eye can reach, the horizon is bounded by a low range of purple-colored hills.

This beautiful valley has been the frequent scene of lawless incursions from the rebel outlaws, and the inhabitants, before the arrival of the Union army in the vicinity, were kept in a continued state of trepidation and alarm. The people are mostly Union in their sentiments, there being but three secesh in this whole region of country. Bands of outlaws frequently came down from Cassville, and would rob the Union men of everything in the house—blankets, bread and bacon. If they caught the owner, he would be taken under guard to Cassville, where he would be tried before a self-constituted vigilance committee.

The head of this committee was the notorious "Joe Peevy," former Sheriff of Barry county. This Peevy was a terror to the whole country. He is resolute, brave, and a man of great and indomitable energy. He seems to have been governed in his actions by a spirit of rude justice, which he administered alike to friend and foe. His capture and imprisonment at Cassville, by our men, gave great satisfaction to the people everywhere.

General Curtis, while passing through Keitsville, had planted a Union flag on one of the houses in town, and this man Peevy, a few days afterwards, took it down, and carried it off. In a few days, therefore, some of our boys came across him, in the timber, and brought him to Cassville, under guard.

Joe Peevy came down through this valley, last summer, with a squad of his lawless jay-hawkers, and got a handsome drubbing by the hardy mountaineers, under Charles Galloway and "Old Jimmy Moore," at Clark's Mill, on Flat Creek. Only one Union man, by the name of Boyce, was killed, while twelve of the rebels were left on the field *hors du combat*. A man named Jeff. Hudson was waylaid, last week, by a party of secesh, and fired upon. He was hit in the toe, but returned the fire on his pursuers, while falling back, and made his escape. Another young man, named James

Reeves, was shot at, while returning home, the other evening, near Jenkins' Creek.

The farms through this valley, in the neighborhood of the main roads, are laid waste. Fences are burned up, and buildings are deserted, and torn to pieces. No preparations are being made for putting in spring crops by the few farmers yet remaining here.

> "To mute, and to material things,
>   New life revolving summer brings;
>   The gentle call dead nature hears,
>   And in her glory re-appears.
>   But O! this country's winter state,
>   What second spring shall renovate."

The evening of the 8th found the regiment encamped at a place called "Cape Fair," in Stone county, Missouri. It reached this "God-forsaken" place after having marched over a broken range of mountains, of some twenty-five miles, since morning. The direct distance would not exceed twelve miles, to the old camp, but, owing to the circuitous windings of the road, it was increased two-fold.

No one can have an adequate idea of the picturesque scenery, and wild alpine views, which everywhere greets the eye of the traveler in this section of the State.

The road passes along the winding crests of a successive range of mountains, frequently curving around, and doubling, so that, in many places, the head of the column seemed to be marching to the rear, and to be within speaking distance of the troops two or three miles behind. Occasionally the eye would overlook profound gorges, of seemingly impenetrable depth, anon broad valleys would appear on either side, and the blue tops of mist-covered mountains be seen away to the north, as far as Springfield, or shutting in the horizon, on the south, far beyond the Arkansas line, some sixteen miles distant. This noble scenery extorted frequent expressions of surprise and admiration from the most indifferent spectator of the sublime in natural scenery. We frequently saw those singular looking hills, often met in Missouri, covered with a white, flinty rock, as if sown broad-cast, giving the landscape an appearance as if whitened by a snow-storm, or a shower of ashes.

We passed through a portion of the extensive "pinery," from which lumber of a fine quality is procured, and transported for building material to various parts of the State. The day was cloudy, and the melancholy murmur of the breeze through the "pine tree's wavy top," added to the sombre character of our march. Not a house was to be seen, nor did we meet with but one solitary passenger, who, of course, was taken in hand by each successive officer, and subjected to an *ex-parte* examination. The desolate condition of the region passed was hit off by a cavalry-man, who volunteered the opinion "that a blue-jay, in flying over, would have to carry a haversack, lashed to his wings, or starve." The assertion would certainly be true of a "blue-jayhawker."

Cape Fair, where we are encamped, has a few windowless huts, situated in the bend of Flat Creek. The latter stream, which bubbles up out of the ground at Cassville, is here anything but flat. The stream, like the "arrowy Rhone," pours an angry, black volume past here, as it comes down from the mountains, and, at this period of the year, is swollen so as to be impassable, except to horses or boats. Flat Creek empties

(8)

into James River, a mile below this point. The latter stream is so much swollen, by the recent freshets, that fording is impracticable, and the army, it is thought, will have to rest here several days, unless the stream, some three miles below, at Mr. Carr's, is fordable.

Had Price been a few miles on the other side, it would not have taken the army long to have found a way of crossing over.

In coming from Springfield the streams were not an impediment. The cavalry were invariably in the advance, with some mountain howitzers, and, whenever they could come within shelling distance of the enemy, they threw some shells at them. The report of the guns would come back over the hills to the column of infantry, and then the order would surely be sent along the line to double-quick. The column would move off, for a mile or two, on double-quick, and if a stream, large or small, was to be crossed, no halt would be made, but "forward" was the word, and the stream was crossed. This stream would have been crossed, in the same way, had the enemy been in the front. Fortunately there was no great emergency, as it was rather uncertain where the enemy would spring up. Rumors were unreliable, and positive information could not be had as to Price's whereabouts. A force was known to be at Forsyth, but how large, or of what importance, no one seemed to know; yet it was important that the army should be on the move, as this was an out-of-the-way place, and rations might soon become scarce. How was the river to be crossed? Some suggested one plan, and some another. But the ingenuity of some one suggested a bridge of wagons for the troops to march over on. Wagons were, therefore, placed in line, from one shore to the other, and boards laid over the tops of the wagon beds. This made an excellent bridge for footmen, and, by four o'clock of the 9th, the army was all over, and in camp on the opposite shore.

The march was continued the next morning, and the evening of the 10th witnessed the camping of the army on the east bank of Big Bear River, forty-eight miles from Cassville.

The streams in this country are most beautiful. They are not large, nor deep, but of very rapid current. Their waters, excepting after heavy rains, when they become thickened by the washings from the mountains, are as clear as the purest crystal. They are fed by springs from the mountain gorges, and these are so numerous as to increase the small rivulet to a good-sized stream, within the distance of a few miles.

The march, at one time, was down a narrow ravine, at the head of which was issuing, from under an overhanging rock, a small spring. In following down the ravine, this stream was crossed several times, and each crossing developed a largely increased stream, when, at the last crossing, not five miles from the first little spring, the water was up to the axle-trees of the wagons, and at least twenty feet in width, and large fish were seen swimming beneath its pellucid surface.

On the morning of the 11th, the regiment pitched tents at the foot of one of the rugged Ozark mounts, that overlook the small valley of Big Bear River. The camp is named "Good News," because here was received the news of the capture of Island Number Ten, by General Pope. It is ten miles from Forsyth, in Taney county, Missouri.

An incident of exceeding interest occurred here on the afternoon of Sunday, the 13th. It was no less than the delivery of a sermon by the Chaplain of the regiment.

Dr. Hazlett had returned to the regiment while it lay at Cassville, and was now in charge—Doctor Maynard being still detained with the wounded at Leetown. On the evening of the arrival in camp here, the wagons were not all up, in consequence of bad roads, and Doctor Hazlett was without blankets. Lieutenant Brasher, Quartermaster of the regiment, was a particular friend of the Doctor's, and proffered to lend him blankets for the night. The Doctor sent his orderly, and had a nice bed made. Being very tired, he soon fell asleep, and slept soundly for two or three hours. Something now seemed to disturb his slumbers; he became restless; a crawling sensation pervaded his skin, and the inclination to scratch was irresistible. From this time forward there was no more rest for the Doctor. Some two hours earlier than was his custom he arose from his couch, unrefreshed, and in bad humor. After sick-call he retired to ascertain the cause of his peculiar sensations. The fact soon became patent that he was literally covered with "body-guard," (army lice.) "Hell and furies, Chris., look at these blankets, and see what's on them!" was his immediate orders to Chris. An examination showed them full of body-lice. "Carry them out, and burn the d—d things!" and out the Doctor rushed, in search of the Quartermaster

"Brasher, did you know that those blankets you loaned me last night were filled with lice?"

"Why, no; were they?" says Brasher, very innocently. "Well, now, maybe they were, for my negro has been using them for the last month."

The Doctor's anger was great, but he manfully swallowed it, and received the joke, and a bottle of whisky, with the best grace possible. There was no man in the regiment who prided himself so much in having neat clothing, and a cleanly person, as Doctor Hazlett, and this, perhaps, was the only time he had ever been tormented by these "plebian tormentors."

CHAPTER XVII.

On the morning of the 16th of April, the regiment broke camp on Bear River, re-crossed it, and filed off up its western bank, until it came to Bull Run, then up Bull Run fifteen miles, to Bull's Mills, when it again went into camp. In coming up the run, it was necessary for the boys to wade it nineteen times. One man in particular, was compelled to take it, deep or shallow, because of some previous misconduct. He was tied to the tail-gate of a wagon, and thus trudged all day "*nolens volens.*" Tying men behind wagons, on the march, is a favorite way of punishing the soldier for trivial offences.

The encampment is now in a small valley, entirely shut in by mountains, excepting the narrow gorge through which Bull Run finds its way to Bear River. From where the writer sits, the view is beautiful. Many of the trees on the opposite mountain side, are clothed in their summer garb, and many are only putting on their vestments of green, with sear and yellow leaves exposed beneath. Here is one green as can be, just beyond, is another red with flowers of the red bud, and then another, as white as the driven snow, with dogwood blossoms. Now is a spot of green earth, and just above it hangs a heavy mass of moss-grown rock, threatening the destruction of this magnificent scenery, by its speedy fall. Flowers of many kinds, are blooming everywhere around. Sweet Williams, Johny-jump-up's and blue bells are abundant, and lend enchantment to the view.

At the foot of this mountain slope, are the white tents of the regiments. The blue smoke of their camp fires, is apparently climbing the mountain, giving a peculiar shade to the picture. Soldiers are everywhere mingled in the scene, some are busy cooking, some sitting or lying down, some walking, and *there* is an officer on horseback. To the right is the mill and the dwelling house of the miller. Close by the mill, are some soldiers, fishing, and they complete the scene, as presented on the 18th day of April, 1862.

Some excitement was created in camp, on the morning of the 19th, by the appearance of three very indignant ladies from the country, seeking Colonel Frederick's head-quarters, for the purpose of entering complaint against two boys of the Fifty-Ninth, for creating a disturbance at their house the night before, and sleeping with two of these ladies "*nolens volens.*" The other, the mother of the two younger ladies, was on the hunt of a cavalry man, who was guilty of some offense against her. These boys were arrested and court-martialed. Two were convicted and one acquitted. The two convicted ones, were summarily drummed out of service with shaved heads.

The Division broke up camp again on the 20th, and moved out in the rain and over the muddiest roads imaginable. They marched this day twenty miles, without anything to eat from the time of starting, until going into camp, and many of the boys had no supper the night before.

At West Plains, some fifty of the Fifty-Ninth, were detached to report under Captain Elliott, to the gun-boat fleet, then laying at Cairo, for duty. They left the regiment about the 25th of April, from which time, they spent the remainder of their term of service on the water. From West Plains, the regiment proceeded to Sulphur Rock, arriving there on the 8th of May.

On the 10th of May, the Fifty-Ninth Illinois, Twenty-Second Indiana, and the Twenty-Fifth and Thirty-Fifth Illinois regiments, being detached from General Curtis's command, started "en route" for Cape Girardeau, Missouri. After marching nine days out of ten, these regiments arrived at the Cape on the evening of the 20th of May; having marched two hundred and fifty miles in ten days, resting one. On the morning of the 20th, the Fifty-Ninth started in the rear of the column. They were some thirty-five miles from the Cape, and all very anxious to arrive at their destination. The Twenty-Second Indiana was next ahead of the Fifty-Ninth, and equally as eager to make the Cape that day. It was a hard march, and about sundown all the regiments had bivouacked, except the Twenty-Second and Fifty-Ninth. These pulled ahead and passed the others some mile or two, when the Twenty-Second caved in. The Fifty-Ninth pushed on and came out nearest the Cape, and went into camp, exultant over their grey-hound perseverance.

These regiments, on their arrival at Cape Girardeau, presented a "war worn" and rugged appearance. Some were entirely destitute of shoes, some had no coats, some were without hats, and many possessed only the remnants of pantaloons. Teams were immediately sent off to town for clothing and rations, and by the next evening, the men scarcely knew themselves in their new uniform.

The 23d was a bright fair day, and Colonel Frederick

priding himself exceedingly on the fine appearance of his regiment, determined to exhibit them to the admiring gaze of the citizens of the Cape. At nine o'clock, they left camp and marched to town, arriving in town the band struck up a lively march, and the steady tramp of the boys, to the time of the music, attracted the attention of the multitude. After marching through several streets, the regiment stacked arms and proceeded by companies, to the Paymaster's office, to receive their pay. After getting paid, the regiment fell into line and marched to the landing, where a steamboat was in waiting, to take them on board. This was the first indications of a ride, since leaving the old War Eagle, at Boonville. Since then, the regiment had marched twelve hundred miles, and now to be transported was quite a treat.

At five o'clock, on the 23d, the boat left the camp for Hamburg landing. When opposite Paducah, Governor Yates, of Illinois, from the guards of another boat, addressed a few congratulatory and cheering remarks to the Fifty-Ninth, "upon what had transpired while they were out in the wilderness." Arriving at Hamburg landing on the 25th, the regiment went into camp some two miles from the river, out towards Corinth.

Humburg is the landing for all of General Halleck's army supplies, at this time, and the scene about the landing, is a lively one. Boats are coming up and un loading their cargoes daily. Mules, horses, wagons, rations, &c., are everywhere lumbering up the bluffs. From the boats the supplies are loaded into wagons, and forwarded to the army now before Corinth. Here are still seen many of the effects of the late battle. Here are the bluffs from which it is said many of our *brave* boys threw themselves into the river, to escape from the pursuing enemy." "Brave boys were they." Here the regiment was furnished with a new outfit of camp equipage, wagons and horses.

Corinth was now supposed to be their destination, and in confirmation, the march towards that place was commenced on the morning of the 27th. The country from Hamburg landing to Corinth, is an unbroken wild, level and swampy. After a march of sixteen miles, over a recently constructed military road, the regiment went into camp about three miles to the north of Corinth.

After the battle of Pea Ridge, P. Sidney Post obtained leave of absence, until his wound should so far heal, as to permit of active service. *Here* he rejoined the regiment as Colonel of the same, having received a commission during his absence. Lieut. Colonel C. H. Frederick, after having commanded the regiment for nine months, with honor to himself and credit to the regiment, now resigned his command to Colonel Post, and very soon, thereafter, received and accepted an appointment on General Jeff. C. Davis' staff.

On the morning of the 28th, the regiment moved into position before the works of the enemy, leaving the tents standing, and the camp equipage all in camp. Some skirmishing was occurring occasionally, between our pickets and those of the enemy, but no fighting of any consequence.

The evacuation of Corinth, by the rebels, commenced on the 28th, so at least it was reported around camp, and so it was believed by several of the Division commanders; but General Halleck either discredited it or did not wish to encourage such an idea. General Pope was satisfied of the fact, and solicited the privilege of moving his command into a position that would prevent their escape; but was refused the request, with the reply that they could not escape. Large trees in elevated positions, had been selected and trimmed, and "look outs" stationed on the tops of these, so that the movements of the rebels could be seen in Corinth. These "look outs" confirmed the reports of the evacuation. No efforts were, however, made to prevent it. General Halleck's army all lay quietly behind their breastworks, to the north of town, leaving the way for the enemy to escape, entirely open; whereas, a small force could have been sent to prevent it and with General Halleck's army, the whole rebel army could have been captured. This was seen and believed by nearly all the privates in the army; yet on the morning of the 30th, Corinth was in our possession without a fight, *and nothing else.*

The vast army, that General Halleck had been for months collecting, from all parts of the country at an enormous expense, and the great amount of labor and suffering of this vast army had all been in vain—entirely useless. Corinth and the whole territory left in our possession, was entirely worthless. And all this because Beauregard would not remain in Corinth until Halleck could dig his way under his fortifications and blow him up.

As soon as the rebels, with all their material, were out of danger from our troops, a forward movement was ordered. Great and universal disappointment was manifested by the whole army when the fact was known that the rebels were all gone. Many and bitter were the curses against General Halleck. Every man felt that it was by his incapacity, want of energy, or a good feeling towards the rebel army, that they escaped so easily. All confidence was lost in the capacity of General Halleck as a commander, and it has never been restored by any of his subsequent official acts. There has been two great errors committed by some body during this war. The one was the removal of Fremont from the command at Springfield, Mo., and the other is the placing Halleck in command of the army before Corinth.

The fortifications about Corinth were found to be trivial, in comparison to what was expected. One line of breast works of weak construction, and nothing but a few slight embrasures comprised the whole thing. Such fortifications one year afterwards, would have been looked upon as no impediment to the advance of our army.

On the 30th, the Fifty-Ninth Illinois again broke camp, and moved out ten miles below Corinth, where they awaited the reconstruction of a bridge, which the rebels had burned. Cannonading is occasionally heard in the distance, which indicates that our advance is skirmishing with the rear of the flying enemy. Camp is pitched near Boonville, Miss., and on the morning of the 2d of June, the regiment moves out on a scout, leaving every thing but their blankets and haversacks in camp. Those unable to march are left in charge of an officer, to guard the camp, and the sick are left in the care of the Hospital Steward. The regiment pursued the enemy about twenty miles without overtaking them, and then returned to camp. It now lay in camp ten days without molestation. The enemy had fled beyond pursuit for the time being, but was still in hearing distance of our scouts, and the anticipation of another move was daily increasing. Instead of pursuing the enemy, the regiment returned to within two miles of Corinth, on the 12th, and went into regular camp on

Clear Creek. There having been no rain for two weeks, the roads were now very dusty, and the marching very disagreeable; consequently it was a pleasant thing to go into camp on the shady banks of a clear stream of running water.

This weather is delightful; only when the sun is at the meridian, then it is a little too hot for comfort. The early morning in camp is delightful, especially. The sun is just peeping up through the tree-tops. The birds are singing their early matins, before the smoke of camp becomes too thick for their vocal organs. The mules are adding their musical braying for their feed of dry oats, and the drivers are aiding the mules with their morning notes of universal cursing. To arise these mornings and witness all this, is charming.

The boys are now having easy, good times. They have plenty of leisure to lay in the shade, and write letters to their friends at home. Policing of camp grounds in the morning, is all that is required of them, and this is usually done by extra-duty men. These are lazy fellows who will not get up in the morning in time to answer to their names at roll call. As a punishment, they are used as scavengers for the benefit of the industrious ones.

There is considerable sickness amongst the men at this time, owing, perhaps, to the hot, dry weather, and bad water of this region. There are some nice springs along Clear Creek, but as a general thing, the only drinking water the men have had since leaving the Tennessee River, has been obtained from the marshes which here abound. All this region of country around Corinth, is a low, swampy, worthless marsh. Why, in the name of common sense, the rebel army was ever molested in the peaceable possession of Corinth is more than can now be comprehended. Why not have left them here; that they might starve, or sicken and die after their own liking.

There are some very noisy fellows in camp, and it seems as though they are always making the most noise when respect for others should keep them most quiet. There are two good brass bands in the immediate neighborhood of our regiment, which frequently dispense most delightful music—but many times these rude fellows are like the dog in the manger, they will neither listen themselves, or let any one else enjoy the music. They are just the kind of men for an army, though—for a "man who has no music in his soul, is fit for treasons, stratagems and spoils."

The boys have many ways of amusing themselves while laying in camp, and some of these they put into practice here. The most profitable and interesting of all others, is the attendance on the prayer meetings, the Chaplain is now conducting in the regiment. The Rev. Shoemate has been with the regiment since its organization, and has preached some three times since leaving Boonville, and is now having the first prayer meetings. These sermons and meetings have only cost the government the moderate sum of two hundred and fifty dollars each. An active, energetic and christian Chaplain is of invaluable service to the army, but an unconverted Chaplain is a nuisance. If there is any place on God's fair earth, where wickedness "stalketh abroad in daylight," it is in the army. It is lamentable to hear and see the profanity and wickedness which every where and all the time meets the ear and eye. Ninety-nine men out of every hundred are profane swearers. Gambling is not quite so universal, yet there are hundreds of young men who devote all their leisure time to this nefarious practice. Walk through camp at almost any hour, and you will see squads of young men engaged in risking their money and their souls on the chance throw of the die. This game is called "chuck-a-luck." A faithful, working christian Chaplain, would, in a great measure, control these practices among the young men of the army.

While at Cross Timbers, in Arkansas, Captain Kelly, of company F, resigned his commission, on account of ill health, and returned to his home in Illinois. Captain Kelly was invariably inclined to be kind and generous towards his men, even to the sacrifice of his own comfort, and his departure was regretted by all. As a testimony of the regard and esteem which the officers of the regiment had for Captain Kelly, the following "expression" was handed to him by the Major, whose name heads the list of signers:

"We, the officers of the Fifty-Ninth Illinois Volunteer Regiment, take this method of expressing our esteem of Captain S. W. Kelly, as an officer and as a gentleman. In camps and on the march, as his health and strength permitted, his duties were always promptly and faithfully attended to. On the battle field he was firm and unflinching. In retiring to private life, he bears with him our best wishes." Signed J. C. Winters, and by twenty other officers of the regiment.

On the resignation of Captain Kelly, the command of company F devolved on Lieutenant John Kelly. The Lieutenant had faithfully filled the position from that time until now, and was justly entitled to a commission as Captain of the company. This, however, he failed to receive. Lieutenant Curry, of company C, of the same regiment, obtained the commission, and took command of the company after its arrival at Jacinto,

Miss. By the resignation of Captain Taylor, of company H, Lieutenant A. Anthony, was left in command of *that* company. More fortunate than Lieutenant Kelly, he subsequently obtained a Captain's commission and commanded the company as such, until ill health compelled him also to resign.

On the 20th of June, the regiment received orders to move out towards Jacinto, Miss., without tents or baggage, and to leave the sick, cripples and convalescents behind. It marched some twenty miles and bivouacked within two or three miles of Jacinto. Here they remained until the 28th. On the 26th, orders were received at camp to remove the sick to General Field hospital at Corinth, and bring forward the tents and other camp equipage to the regiment. This was accomplished in good order; the trains reporting to the regiment about eleven o'clock, on the 28th. While laying in camp, sickness had increased considerably, and now there was quite a number to be left at hospital. When the train arrived at the regiment, it was under marching orders and making preparations to move. Rations were being distributed to the men, and the Surgeons were drawing a supply of medicines and other hospital stores for their respective regiments. All the indications were that a long and rapid march was in contemplation, or else an engagement with the enemy. Old soldiers are not often deceived in their prognosis.

CHAPTER XVIII.

At three o'clock of the 28th, the regiment again started on the march. Rumor had it that the destination was Holly Springs, which is thirty-five miles south of Memphis. The roads were now in good condition. The dust was nicely settled by a previous rain, and the weather was not so excessively hot as it had been a few days before. The men were well rested, and in good health and spirits. The teams were in good condition, and all seemed propitious for a successful campaign.

Passing through Jacinto, towards Rienzi, the regiment made eight miles, and went into camp. The next morning, starting early, it made fifteen miles, and went into camp one-half mile east of the town of Ripley.

This is quite a pretty town, of, perhaps one thousand inhabitants. It is the county town of Tippah County, Mississippi, and is prettily situated in the best portion of the country the regiment had visited. This was Sunday, and the citizens were all at church when our army made its appearance. The minister was reading a hymn when our advance was first descried, and some one at the church door sang out, the "Yankees are coming!" It may be supposed that this created some alarm—perhaps as much as the cry of fire would have done. The congregation rushed for the door, and, as fast as they could get out of the house, skedaddled—some for their homes, but most of them for the timber, on double-quick. It can easily be believed that there was some tall running about this time. They were taken entirely by surprise. The rebel soldiers that had been there, a few days before, were all gone to some other point, and their withdrawal had caused the citizens to suppose that the town of Ripley was in perfect security; but now, of course, they expected, if caught, to be roasted, and eaten by the cannibal Yankees. Our army, however, marched through the town in perfect good order, molesting no one, nor touching a thing belonging to any one.

A few negroes, three or four old men, and some children, were all that could be seen in the streets, as our soldiers passed.

"Yah, yah, yah; Massa said you 'uns would neber come dis here way—yah, yah." Thus said an old darkey, as we passed him. "He was mistaken dat time, for here you is, sure 'nough—yah, yah."

"Where is your master now?" asked one of our boys.

"He's done gone. Wen you 'uns was seen comin', he broke for de brush—yah, yah."

Monday being muster day, the army lay in camp until Tuesday morning, to allow time for making up the muster-rolls.

The women, and some of the male citizens, had returned to their homes, as soon as they ascertained that the Yankees were not particularly fond of roasted rebels, and many of the officers became domesticated at their houses. At one of these houses an officer was talking with the lady, in the parlor, when a private stepped to the door, to make some inquiry. There was in the parlor at the time, quite a pretty, smart-looking girl, ten or twelve years old, who was attentively listening to the conversation. When the soldier came to the door, the mother pointed towards him, and said to the girl:

"Look there, Eliza. There's a Yankee. You was just asking what kind of an animal they were."

The girl looked at the soldier with astonishment, for a second, then, turning to her mother, said:

"Why, mother, that's not a Yankee; that's a *man*."

This poor girl had expected to see a wild animal of some kind. She had no idea that the Yankees were men. This is in kind with the ignorance of a young woman, whose husband was in the rebel army. She was, herself, a most rabid secesh. Some of our boys were telling her of the victories they had gained over the rebels, particularly the one at Pea Ridge, in Arkansas. "O, yes," said she, "you whipped us there; but you never could have done it if it had'nt been for the gun-boats." Gun-boats at Pea Ridge, more than ninety miles from water! What an idea! Ignorance is not always bliss.

Tuesday morning, the army again moved out, passing back through Ripley, and on towards Holly Springs. Here Colonel P. Sidney Post came very near being captured. Many of the young "bloods" of the army were in the habit of leaving their commands, and taking up their quarters at citizens' houses whenever an opportunity of the kind offered, on the march, or while in camp. Colonel Post had here formed the acquaintance of some secesh ladies, and enjoyed himself hugely in their society. When the regiment left town, he remained behind a short time to have a parting word with the sweet charmers, and would, perhaps, have remained some time longer had not an acquaintance rode to the door, and urged him to go on with the command. The plot laid to capture him was just completed as he rode away. These fair ladies had made arrangements with some half-dozen rebels to come to the house, and lay in wait, until notified of the opportune moment for their purpose. One of these ladies left the presence of the Colonel for that object, just as the Colonel was urged to go to his command. Five minutes later, and he would have been a prisoner.

Soon after leaving town, two of our boys, who were some distance in the rear of the regiment, on account of ill health, were unexpectedly ordered to halt. On looking around, they discovered some half-dozen guerrillas by the roadside, with guns pointing toward them, in threatening attitude. "Halt! you damned Yankee sons-of-bitches, or we'll blow your brains out," was the order of the rebs. The boys were in a ravine, with hills in front and rear; and, just at this time, there were none of our men in sight. There was no alternative but to surrender. This they did, with as good grace as possible. They were taken some distance from the road, and whatever of value they had was taken from them. A consultation was then held among the captors, to determine whether these two "Yanks" should be shot on the "spot," or taken to General Price, who was then at Tupelo. One or two were for shooting them at once, and thus save trouble; but the majority opposed it, and they were marched off in a southerly direction. They marched until nearly night, when they came to an encampment of rebels, near some small town, the name of which they did not learn. Here they were placed in an old deserted house, together with a number of other prisoners.

The names of these two men were Joseph H. Sullivan

and Jesse L. McHatton. They were soon joined by Moses T. Anderson, captured about the same time, and in the same manner. These three belonged to the Fifty-Ninth Regiment. The other prisoners were from different regiments. There was one prisoner there who had been captured at the siege of Corinth. He was Chaplain to some regiment, and was now under sentence of death, for being a spy. He was a Southern man, with Union sentiments, and hence the supposition that he was a spy for the Union army. He had just had his court-martial, and the sentence was to be put in execution on the morrow. During the evening he told his story to the boys of the Fifty-Ninth, and at once enlisted their sympathies in his behalf. A plan was soon devised, and suggested by Joseph Sullivan, by which he, perhaps, might make his escape. The night happened to be most favorable, and the plan succeeded admirably. There were no lights about the building, consequently all was in darkness as soon as the daylight disappeared. Before that time, however, Joseph Sullivan had noticed a comparatively loose board in the floor, and that the house was considerably raised from the ground, by being set on blocks at the corners.

The plan then was, that the Chaplain should hold prayer-meeting, about nine or ten o'clock, and, while the praying and singing was attracting the attention of the guards, the board in the floor should be taken up, and the Chaplain pass through under the floor, and there remain until he should hear a slight thumping on the floor above him, when he should crawl out at the north-west corner, and make his escape. The Chaplain gave out the hymn from memory, offered up a most excellent and fervent prayer, asking forgiveness on his to-morrow's executioners, and pardon for the whole rebel Confederacy, and praying that they might soon see the error of their ways, and return to their allegiance, etc. He then gave out another hymn, and, while it was being sung, slipped through the opening to the ground beneath the floor. The board was carefully replaced, and all soon became quiet. In about an hour Joseph Sullivan and McHatton, leaving Anderson to give the signal on the floor, used some strategy to attract the attention of the guard, so that the Chaplain had an opportunity to pass out undiscovered. It is not known that he was ever re-captured. The supposition is that he made good his escape, and is now with his friends.

The next morning the prisoners were started on for Tupelo. Arriving at Price's head-quarters, they were ordered to Mobile; from Mobile they were sent to Macon, Georgia, where they were kept until the 8th of October, when they were shipped to Richmond, Virginia, for exchange.

While at Macon, Joseph Sullivan was granted the privilege of the city, that he might work at his trade. He was a shoemaker by trade, and made shoes for the benefit of the sick in hospital. The money he received for his work he expended for quinine, and other necessaries, for the sick prisoners. In this way he accomplished a great amount of good, and will ever be remembered by those thus benefitted with gratitude. These three men were reasonably well treated while prisoners, and returned, September 8, 1864, to their old regiment, in good health.

The march of the regiment was continued, in the direction of Holly Springs, until late in the evening. Reveille at three, and march at five o'clock, is the order for the following morning. True to orders, at five o'clock the regiment is on the move. The march is continued all day, and until one o'clock at night. The men are very tired, and take no time to prepare coffee, but stretch themselves on the ground, and go to sleep. At four o'clock orders came to fall in. Most of the men are yet asleep, but the order must be obeyed, and slowly they fall into ranks. No supper, no breakfast, and yet must march. 'Tis hard, but "Forward, march!" The column moves out, and takes the back track. The enemy is threatening the rear, and will cut us off from our supplies. Hungry and weary, the men drag the march along all day, and go into bivouac ready to pull out again at a moment's notice. We are now not far from Rienzi, having made over sixty miles since the morning of the 1st. The men are on less than half rations, and the teams without forage. Many of the horses were without feed for forty-eight hours, and many of the men, for twenty-four hours, did not have a mouthful of nourishment. This is the heaviest marching the regiment has ever done.

On the 4th the army went into camp at Jacinto, the Fifty-Ninth camping about two miles from town. Although the three days' marching had been very trying on the nerve and muscle of the men, the regiment came into camp at Jacinto in good condition. The health of the regiment was never better. There were very few who had failed to keep their places in the ranks. One man had been severely wounded by the upsetting of a wagon. He was riding on the wagon, asleep, when the driver, in going down a hill, upset his wagon, throwing the sleeper from the comfortable quarters he was enjoying to the earth. An axe being his companion on the wagon, struck his foot as he fell, making a severe wound.

CHAPTER XIX.

Jacinto is a pretty little town, twenty-five miles south of Corinth, in Nishamingo County, and is situated in a cultivated part of the country. As a general thing, this is an uncultivated region. From Corinth through Ripley to within a few miles of Holly Springs, wherever the regiment has marched, the country is comparatively a wilderness. In the immediate vicinity of Rienzi, Jacinto and Ripley, there are some small plantations under ordinary good cultivation. The land is poor and rather unproductive, yielding but small compensation for the labor required to till it. The appearances of the few women and children which are seen along the march, indicates the prevalence of agues and fevers during the spring and fall seasons of the year, and the many swamps and marshes seen in all directions, confirm the supposition that it is a very unhealthy country. The country around Jacinto and the other little towns is more elevated and broken, and affords some assurance of health. Jacinto is in a comparatively healthy location, and should the army remain here during the heat of summer, it may enjoy good health. The water is obtained from springs, and is much more healthy than the brackish water of the swamps, which the soldier was compelled to drink while on the march.

It is now probable that active operations will be suspended till the hot season is over, and the troops are busy making preparations to enjoy a recuperative season in camp. They are determined to have camp as attracting as possible, and as comfortable as green shades and good bunks can make it. The camp grounds of the Fifty-Ninth has been judiciously selected on one of the small pine ridges which skirt the streams of this region, and is convenient to both fence rails and water. Fence rails make most excellent fires for cooking and the cool spring water is a luxury much to be prized during the hot days of this season of the year. The small pine shrubbery affords excellent material for the construction of shades and arbors to protect against the scorching rays of the sun. Some of the companies are taking great pains in the construction of arbors adjoining their tents. Company K has excelled all the others in artistic skill and ingenuity in the construction of these shades. All over camp these bowers are so constructed as to effectually shield from the scorching rays of Old Sol, and groups of hardy looking soldiers are now to be seen engaged in every conceivable pastime, unconscious of the oppressive heat outside. Some are discussing the conservative policy of General Halleck in pittying the rebels—guarding their property from molestation by our soldiers while on the march and while laying in camp, and in feeding the families of those in arms against us from our scant rations.

A squad of men has just left camp to go a mile out, for the purpose of guarding a rebel family against intrusion by any of the soldiers. This, the majority of the disputants are opposed to, while some are in favor of the policy. Some of these boys have been compelled very much against their will, to stop while on the march, and stand guard at the gate of some fine mansion, whose owner was in the rebel army, while the families occupying the log houses along the road were left to the mercy of every straggler in the army. This is looked upon by those opposed to the policy as great injustice.

Some are engaged in writing letters to their friends at home, and some in playing cards, some are reading, and here is a squad attracted by the exciting game of chuck-a-luck. Some are rubbing up their muskets and others are stretched upon their beds of pine, taking a nap. This will continue to be the daily camp scene until orders come to move out again.

Soon after coming into camp, Dr. H. J. Maynard reported from Cassville, Mo., and again took charge of the sick. Dr. Hazlett assumed the duties of Brigade Surgeon, and located himself at Jacinto. As is always the case, while laying in camp, sickness now increases, so that a large hospital tent is required to shelter the patients. This field hospital is still continued at Corinth, and orders are to send all serious cases up there for treatment. The indications also point towards an early move, and it is not policy to have many sick men with the regiment.

There had been an order for several days, to be ready to move at a moment's notice, but no move was made until the 4th of August. On the 4th, the regiment started out on a scout, as was supposed, leaving the camp standing, as is usual on such occasions. The 4th of August was, perhaps, the hottest day of the season, and the men suffered excessively from the heat. Quite a number fell from the ranks with "sun-stroke," and some expired from its effects. None of the Fifty-Ninth died, but two or three never fully recovered from its impression.

On the 6th, the Acting Quartermaster, Lieutenant H.

W. Hall, received orders to break up camp, and move his train to Iuka, Miss., some twenty miles farther east. The sick were all sent to general field hospital, and about noon the train moved out. Passing through Jacinto, it continued to move until nine o'clock, when it overtook the regiment, in bivouac, some six miles from Iuka. The regiment had thus far returned from its expedition, and bivouaced for the train to come up, so as to be safely escorted to Iuka. There were many guerrillas through the country, and it was unsafe to send the train without a strong guard. Early in the morning the march was continued to Iuka, where the regiment again went into regular camp.

The regimental Sutler did not come through with the train, but waited until the next day. When coming through, on the 8th, with three wagons loaded with goods, and six splendid mules to each wagon, the guerrillas came upon him about five miles from Iuka, and captured two wagons and mules with their drivers, and also one man belonging to the ranks in the regiment. The Sutler, who was on horseback, made his escape, as did also one of the wagons. After taking as many of the goods as they could carry away with them, they set fire to the wagons and burned them. The mules and prisoners were taken to Tupelo. Besides the mules and wagons, the Sutler lost about two thousand dollars worth of goods. The prisoners were taken to General Price. Two of them being citizens, one the driver and the other the Sutler's clerk, were released on parole of honor. The soldier, William Workman, of company F, was released by taking an oath of pseudo alliance to the Confederate government.

As soon as it was known that these guerrillas had committed this outrage, a squad of cavalry was started in pursuit, but too late to overtake them. A short distance from where the wagons were burned, the rebels had taken breakfast that morning, and perhaps concealed themselves there the night before. The family at first denied any knowledge of the affair, but in looking around some of the Sutler's goods were discovered. This settled the matter to the satisfaction of our boys, and they immediately ordered the family to pack up such things as they wished to save from the flames, for their house should never harbor any more guerrillas. Soon the house was emptied of its contents, the Sutler's goods were retaken, and the house shared the fate of the wagons—nothing was left but the ashes.

The regiment on leaving Jacinto, marched in a southern direction about twenty-five miles, to a place called Sand Springs. A large cotton factory and dry goods establishment was in operation there, and a camp of three or four hundred rebels in the vicinity. It was for the purpose of breaking up this establishment that the expedition was undertaken. Several regiments were detailed from the different brigades for that purpose, and General Robert Mitchell was in command. The first night out, the command bivouaced on an old rebel's plantation, some fifteen miles south of Jacinto. In the evening, General Mitchell, with his staff, rode forward in advance of the column to this old planter's house, and was most cordially received and welcomed by the old gentlemen, with true southern hospitality. The General soon discovered which way the wind blew with the old man, and encouraged him in his delusion. He informed the planter that he was General Price, of the Confederate army, and that he wished to camp some of his boys near by, and take up his own quarters at his house for the night. The old gentleman was highly delighted, and generously proffered his house and premises for the accommodation of General Price. By this time it had become the dusk of the evening, and our boys were coming into camp in good order. General Mitchell detained the old planter in conversation so closely that he had no opportunity to discover the difference between our boys and his friends, the rebels. After the General had pumped this old rebel to his entire satisfaction, he retired—but before doing so, had a guard placed around the house, with orders to let no one out or in. Before going to bed the old planter attempted to pass the guard, but was not allowed to do so. He thought rather strange of the proceedings, but submitted with a good grace, and retired to dream of the honor to his house in the entertainment of the great General Price, of the Confederate States army.

He was up in the morning early, and again attempted to pass the guard, with no better success, however. It was now becoming light, and the uniform of the soldiers at the door attracted his attention. His suspicions were aroused.

"Are you a Confederate soldier?" said he to the guard.

"No, sir ee," replied the soldier.

"What are you, then?" said the planter, "and how came you here?"

"I am a Union soldier, and am here by the order of General Mitchell."

"Who is General Mitchell, and where is he?" asked the planter, eagerly.

"General Mitchell commands these regiments out here in your fields, and is now in your house."

"And where are the soldiers of General Price?" inquired the old gentleman.

"To hell, for all I know," replied the soldier, who, not understanding the matter, turned away and walked his beat.

The old man re-entered his room, wondering how it all happened. Pretty soon General Mitchell made his appearance, and greeted the planter with a pleasant "good morning."

"How is it, General, that I see so many Union soldiers out here?"

"Those are my boys out there," says the General, "and I am General Mitchell of the Union army, and not General Price, as you was glad to believe last night. It is now time I was on the move, and you will prepare to go with me. I want you to guide me to the Sand Springs, and if you deceive me in one particular your life shall immediately pay the forfeit."

The old planter was sold, and there was no help for it. Sullenly, but faithfully he obeyed orders, and when the expedition returned he was allowed to remain with his family. The rebels fled at our approach; the factory was destroyed; the store gutted, &c.

CHAPTER XX.

Iuka is a pretty little town twenty-five miles east of Jacinto, Mississippi, and is on the Memphis, and Charleston railroad. It is twenty miles south-east of Corinth, and is pleasantly located. The country is rather better than any we have seen in Mississippi, and the improvements are good. The town has some very fine buildings, for private residences, and one fine large hotel. It has several mineral springs in the neighborhood, which have obtained quite a notoriety for their curative properties. Iron, sulphur and salts, characterize the water of these springs. The chalybeate spring is highly impregnated with the medical properties of iron, and is no doubt admirably adapted to some cases of disease. The sulphur spring is also strongly tinctured with sulphur. On account of these springs, Iuka has been a favorite resort for invalid planters and their families, and perhaps, some day may become a noted "watering place."

The regiment went into camp half a mile south of town, on a pleasant piece of ground, formerly used as a play ground for the scholars of an academy located there. The academy building was yet standing, but had been used as barracks for soldiers, and was very much abused. Doctor Maynard took possession of it now, for the use of the sick.

The regiment had now marched in its advances and

retreats, over two hundred miles since coming to the State of Mississippi, and the men were willing to rest for a short time at Iuka.

Rumor now has it, that one Brigade is to remain here during the balance of the summer. The men are thereby encouraged to erect some more pleasant bowers, to protect themselves from the excessive heat.

A day or two after coming here, two of our boys, while scouting through the country, stopped at a widow womans, and in genuine guerrilla fashion, proceeded to rob her of all the money she had, some forty or fifty dollars. The woman followed them to camp, and reported the affair to the Captain of the company. The boys were arrested, but what punishment they received, deponent saith not.

Two other cases of a similar character, only on a much larger scale, and perhaps with more justice, occurred while laying here. A rich old planter, living about two miles from town, had the reputation of being a rebel, although he remained at home, and apparently minded his own business. General Mitchell, however, supposed him to be a fit subject for arrest, and to have the law of confiscation applied to his property. He, therefore, sent a squad of men, and brought the old man to town, together with horses, mules, wagons, cotton, and negroes, to the amount of twenty thousand dollars. All the property was taken for the benefit of the Government, and the old gentleman was held for the safety of the commonwealth.

The other case was that of an old planter in Alabama, about twenty miles south of Iuka. He, too, was rich, with negroes, cotton, mules, etc., and was tainted with disunion sentiments. General Mitchell deemed it necessary to clip the wings of his riches, also, lest they should fly over to the rebel cause. Accordingly, a detachment of two or three regiments, the Fifty-Ninth included, were started out one evening, about sun-down, to make him a visit. After marching all night, they came to the plantation at sun-rise, or just before, but not early enough to catch the old planter. The negroes, cotton, mules, horses and wagons, were taken in possession. Other plantations were visited, and many bales of cotton were found hid away in the brush, the hiding places being pointed out by the negroes. The expedition returned, with ninety bales of cotton, besides other property, to the amount of several thousands of dollars. These three cases were somewhat similar, but with this difference: the one was in accordance with guerrilla warfare, the other according to the law of civilized warfare.

The health of the regiment continued good while here, although some cases occurred from the excessive use of green corn, and other imprudent indulgences. One patient, (Nathan Logue, of Company B,) was taken sick on the morning of the 18th, was sent to town to general hospital on the morning of the 19th, and died that afternoon, at three o'clock.

The First Lieutenant of Company F, (John Kelly,) was here compelled to leave his company, and attend solely to his own afflictions. For several months his eyes had been affected with severe inflamation, which now became almost insupportable. The Surgeon, (Doctor Maynard,) had frequently advised him to resign his commission, and leave the army, until he could get his eyes restored to a healthy condition. This he persistently refused to do. His love of country was above all considerations of self. Said he: "My country needs my services. I was, also, instrumental in getting the boys of Company F to enlist, and they were generous enough to give me the second position in the company, and now I will not desert them. I will share their toils and hardships as long as it is possible for me to do so." Now his eyes had become so much inflamed that he could not see. The pain was excessive, his whole system became deranged, fever set in, typhoid symptoms soon made their appearance, and he became prostrated. He was taken to a private house in town, was well nursed and medically attended; but nature could endure no longer, and, in August he was buried at Iuka, Mississippi. He was beloved by all belonging to his company, and highly respected by every officer and private in the regiment. His love of country was only excelled by his love of virtue.

CHAPTER XXI.

Orders came to the regiment on the morning of the 18th of August, to march at twelve o'clock. This order had been anticipated for a day or two, and did not create any surprise. Although the men had been expecting to remain some time longer at Iuka, they willingly proceeded to pull down arbors and strike tents. The Fifty-Ninth had been in service long enough to learn that orders were not rumors or suppositions, and that to obey with alacrity was characteristic of a contented soldier; and that, however much they might desire to stay at Iuka, the better policy was to leave without complaint.

"Rumors, rumors; vague, contradictory! Surely, like the heath on which the witches in 'Macbeth' stirred their gruel, and summoned the spirits of many colors." As W. L. F. writes of Memphis, so Iuka is at this time—the gathering place of "black rumors and white, red rumors and grey." Every hour there is a new batch of them. One rumor says that General Buell is now in the Sequatchie Valley, east of Stevenson and north of the Tennessee River, nearly north of Chattanooga, with General Kirby Smith in his front, with Polk and Bragg in his rear, and with Forrest's cavalry on the north, which is large, and another formidable force on the south, leaving him a bare possibility of escaping with his command. Then comes another one on the same day, and tells that General Bragg was near Bolivar, with an army of twenty thousand men, and about to surround General Ross, who is in command at that place. And still another—that "Price is at Grand Junction," and is about to eat up the army of General Rosecranz, at Corinth. To the relief of some one of these points, the command of General Davis is now to be sent. Some suppose it will be back to Corinth, and some to relieve Buell. The latter proved to be the correct supposition, and hence the direction taken was towards Tennessee.

At twelve o'clock, the command moved out. At one o'clock it commenced raining, and continued raining till the next morning. The command marched eight miles that afternoon, going into camp sometime after dark—and dark it was, too. Wet and hungry, the men had to lay that night without fire or tents. It was too dark to find wood, and the wagons did not come up in time to pitch tents. About day-light the rain ceased, and the sun came up bright and cheering, and disclosed to view the small town of Eastport, and the Tennessee River. Two steamboats were in waiting at the wharf to ferry the troops over.

Eastport is on the left bank of the Tennessee River, in the north-east corner of the State of Mississippi. It is, altogether, a one-horse town, although some business in the way of shipping produce has been carried on here. The town is situated on one of those high, abrupt banks, which are everywhere met with along the Tennessee River. The view from the bluff just above town affords a most magnificent scenery. In the east the sun is lending a brilliancy to the dispersing rain-clouds of the night before. In the south the blue waters of the Tennessee, are seen emerging from a narrow avenue, among the heavy foliage of the forest trees, in the distance; and in the north the same waters are seen disappearing as they came, to find their level in the bosom of its rival—the Ohio. Beneath you lay the two steamboats, sending up their wreath of white, and their black columns of smoke. A line of soldiers are forming on the wharf to await the order for crossing. In the back-ground are the camps, with their thousand soldiers, in all conceivable attitudes, giving a lively finish to the picture.

Soon after sun-rise the troops commenced crossing. At three o'clock the Fifty-Ninth crossed over, and went into camp about one mile from the river. The 20th was consumed in getting the trains over, and in fitting up rations, etc., for a continued march. While here the boys amused themselves bathing in the river, and washing up their dirty clothing. Here, too, Colonel Post again came very near being captured. He, with Doctor Maynard, who was ever ready for a scout, or a dash at the Johnny secesh, rode out beyond the lines in the evening, and called at a plantation, where two or three ladies detained them until after dark. Soon after starting for camp they were ordered to "halt" by some unseen foe; but, not being inclined to an ambush, they put spurs to their horses, and made their escape, although several shots were fired after them.

On the morning of the 21st we again broke camp, and did not pitch tents until we reached Florence, Alabama. Florence is a beautiful town, of, perhaps, one thousand inhabitants. It is situated near the right bank of the Tennessee River, not far from the Tennessee State line. It seems to be a place of some business, but, to judge from appearances, it is principally occupied by wealthy citizens, who are destitute of employment. There is no other town so well calculated for the enjoyment of repose as Florence. The houses, for the most part, are set back some distance from the street, and the front yard is filled with most delightful shade trees. Many of these trees are quite large, indicating great age, but have been cut off at the top so as not to be of too great a hight for ornament as well as shade. In riding along the street, in hot weather, the inclination to stop, and take a siesta under these cool shades, is almost irresistable. A glimpse of the white cottage, within, is only now and then obtained through the thick foliage of the trees in front. No wonder the citizens of Florence are opposed to the emancipation policy. To lay in the shade here, and have slaves to wait on you—what more could be desired?

The regiment encamped near the river, not far from a railroad bridge that had been burned by General Sherman, a few months before.

The tents, and all camp equipage, were now ordered to be left behind, and the men march with light knapsacks. From Florence the march was continued to Lawrenceburg, Tennessee; thence to Columbia, from Columbia to Franklin, and through Franklin to Murfreesboro', Tennessee. Here we lay in camp one day, and then moved out for Nashville. Starting late in the evening, we reached Nashville next afternoon at four o'clock, making over thirty miles in less than twenty four hours.

The country, from Florence to Murfreesboro', is under good cultivation, and is the most productive of any the army has passed through since leaving Boonville, Missouri. The splendid plantations of General Polk and brothers are on this road, and are unsurpassed by any that we have ever seen. The buildings are of the most approved style of modern architecture, and the grounds are most beautifully arranged, after the English model. All that money, art and slave labor can accomplish is here displayed. The land is rich, and under a high state of cultivation.

Columbia, Franklin and Murfreesboro' are interesting towns, of twelve or fifteen hundred inhabitants each. At Columbia is an obelisk, erected to the memory of the heroes who volunteered to leave their homes, and the town of Columbia, for the purpose of serving in the Mexican war. The inscriptions on this monument give the names, rank, age and time of death of these honorable heroes. It is quite an ornament to the public square of the town, and speaks volumes in praise of the good and patriotic citizens. The honor was due the Mexican heroes.

The command passed through Franklin on Sunday. The citizens were consequently at leisure to meet on the streets and witness the soldiers as they marched through town. The soldier prides himself, at all times, on his soldierly appearance when in the ranks, but, when passing through these secesh towns, he more than takes delight in showing himself to good advantage. "Here's your Yankee soldier, you insignificant traitor, you—look at him, and tremble"—is the expression he wears on his countenance, and exhibits in his military step and bearing. The citizens of Franklin were much more numerous than had been seen in any of the towns hitherto passed through. There were, perhaps, more union people, and a less number who had fled at our approach.

Five miles west of Franklin a large cotton factory is in operation, and, as the army passed, the factory girls, to the number of two or three hundred, came out to see it pass. The girls were neatly dressed in their holiday clothing, and presented a very interesting spectacle to the soldiers. Many months had passed since so many young ladies had been looked upon by these war-worn soldiers. Home and civilized society was brought to the memory, and many a sad thought forced itself through the mind, of the loved ones at home, who, to-day, were congregated at their places of Sunday gathering, in the country, to hear glad tidings from the preacher. Jests and repartees flew thick and fast between the girls and the soldier-boys, as the regiments moved by. Many of these girls were very pretty and intelligent, although they, more than likely, belonged to the families of the "poor white trash" of the South.

When going into camp near Murfreesboro', two boys of the Fifty-Ninth left the regiment to visit a house half a mile from the road for the purpose of getting something for their supper. While there they were surprised by three or four guerrillas and taken prisoners. News of the affair soon came to camp and a squad was sent out after them, but without success.

Arriving at Nashville on the 4th the regiment went into camp two miles south of the city, and lay there until the morning of the 6th, when it again moved out. Passing through the city it crossed the Tennessee river and encamped near Edgefield. Here General Davis lays in wait until the balance of Buell's army could come up and cross the river. General Jeff. C. Davis was detached from the army of General Rosecranz, at Iuka, with eight thousand men, and reported to General Buell at Murfreesboro'. The Fifty-Ninth Illinois was in his command and was among the first regiments that crossed the river at Nashville.

The positions of General Buell's army at Battle Creek, Huntsville, and McMinnville, on account of the movements of General Bragg's rebel army, became untenable, and had to be evacuated. General Bragg massed his army at Chattanooga and Knoxville, Tennessee. One corps, under General Kirby Smith, had succeeded in a flank movement, and had already reached the borders of Kentucky. Two other corps under General Hardee and Leonidas Polk were about to succeed in joining Smith, thus forming an army of forty thousand men—sufficiently strong to threaten either Cincinnati or Louisville, and cut General Buell off from all his communications. These movements caused General Buell to move his army with all dispatch towards Louisville to secure his own safety and that of Louisville and Cincinnati.

The crossing was effected on the 8th, and about sunset the Fifty-Ninth again pushed out. The evening was mild and pleasant, although somewhat lowering. Clouds were accumulating and thickening in the west, and appearances rather indicated rain. No rain had fallen since leaving Eastport, and the roads were getting very dry and dusty, and water very scarce. A rain would therefore be very acceptable at this time—but such a rain as fell that night was more than agreeable! The troops had hardly got under way, when it became dark, and continually growing darker. It finally became "darkness visible," and the rain commenced. The heavens opened and poured their floods of water in torrents; the lightning's vivid flash is blinding, and the thunder's roar exceeds the combined report of all earth's artillery. No mortal man could march in such a storm, and for half an hour the *mighty* hosts of General Buell bent themselves submissively to the will of Him "who rides upon the whirlwind and controls the storm." When the storm moderated, the march was continued and kept up until two o'clock in the morning. After marching all night, the regiment lay here quietly in camp for over thirty-six hours, and then made another night march, and lay in camp a day. Why this night marching, and laying by through the day, is unaccountable to outsiders.

The march now continues from day to day until the 27th of September, when the army encamps at Louisville. The route traversed by General Jeff. C. Davis' division, was from Nashville via Franklin, Dripping Springs, Cave City, to Bowling Green; from Bowling Green through Mumfordsville, Elizabethtown and West Point to Louisville. The distance from Nashville to Louisville, by the roads marched over, is over two hundred miles, and the time occupied in marching was fourteen days. The army having layed by four days and counter-marched one. At Dripping Springs the division encamped one night, and marched out early the next morning, and until twelve o'clock. A halt was called, the column faced about and marched directly back to the last night's camp. Buell was either a knave or a coward, or perhaps both. The probabilities are that if Buell had marched his army as a *General* should and would have done from Nashville on, he would have saved the surrender of the four thousand brave men at Mumfordsville. But what time he could not loiter away, he took up in counter-marching his weary and half-fed troops.

A division of only two brigades of Bragg's army under General Buckner, attacked our forces at Mumfordsville. This force consisted of the Sixteenth, Seventeenth Sixty-Seventh and Eighty-Third Indiana regiments, under Colonel Wilder. After being repulsed three times, with a loss of two or three hundred, they retire to await reinforcements. In a day or two they renew the attack with a largely increased force. After a desperate resistance, Colonel Wilder is compelled to surrender. The prisoners are paroled, and in a day or two they pass through our columns to the rear, without arms. Why was it that General Buell did not reinforce that bravely defended garrison? If, instead of counter-marching twenty miles and wasting two or three days in idleness, he had steadily advanced with his army, Mumfordsville would have been saved. Had he have been seen and known along the lines at the time those brave men were passing to the rear, his hide would never have held bran.

When our army passed through the ground held by the rebels, during the attack, the dead were yet unburied. A rebel officer and private soldier, the one in splendid uniform, the other in rags, were side by side, awaiting the sexton's aid. From Mumfordsville to Louisville the march was continued unintermittingly, and on less than half rations and some days without water. Some of the men were without food for forty-eight hours. Without shoes, ragged and dirty, they arrive at Louisville, contrasting beautifully with the neatly uniformed recruits about the city, with their paper collars and blacked boots.

General Jeff. C. Davis' division had now marched about three hundred and seventy-five miles since the 18th of August, and over six hundred miles since leaving Corinth, Miss.

The sick and disabled were left in hospital at Bowling Green as the regiment came through, so that on its arrival at Louisville there was but one disabled man in the Fifty-Ninth, and he unfortunately became disabled by falling from the top of a loaded wagon and breaking his arm.

While at Louisville, the boys, as a general thing, had the privilege of the city and enjoyed themselves very much. Some of them took "french leave," and visited their friends over the river. One man, William Rumey, company H, lost his life while here, in an unfortunate difficulty with a fellow soldier. Rumsey was a good soldier, and not at all inclined to be quarrelsome, but through some evil influence he enraged one of General Mitchell's body guard to such a degree that he drew his pistol and shot him.

Here, also, the regiment met with a great loss by the transfer of Dr. H. J. Maynard to another department. Through the influence of some friends in Arkansas, he was commissioned First Surgeon of the First Arkansas Cavalry Regiment. This entitled him to a transfer, and he bid adieu to the Fifty-Ninth Illinois at Louisville. His withdrawal from the regiment was seriously regretted by all who had ever had any intercourse with him. As a man, he was affable and gentlemanly in his intercourse with the men, and as a Surgeon, he was courteous, kind and scientific. His liberality and goodness of heart endeared him to all in the regiment. He will ever carry with him the respect and gratitude of all those to whom he ministered while with the command.

The most *striking* incident which occurred while the regiment lay at Louisville, was the shooting of General Nelson by Jeff. C. Davis. It is to be hoped that the act was morally and legally justifiable.

General Jeff. C. Davis was at home on leave of absence, which he obtained a short time before his division left the State of Mississippi, on a plea of ill health. When the alarm was raised in Louisville that the enemy were marching on that city, General Jeff. C. Davis, who could not reach his command under General Buell, then at Bowling Green, went to General Nelson and tendered his services. General Nelson gave him the command of the city militia, so soon as they were organized. General Davis opened an office and went to work in assisting in the organization. On Wednesday, General Davis called upon General Nelson in his room at the Galt House, in Louisville, when the following took place:

General Davis said, "I have the brigade, General, you assigned me, ready for service, and have called to inquire if I can obtain arms for them."

General Nelson—"How many men have you?"

General Davis—"About twenty-five hundred men, General."

General Nelson—roughly and angrily—"About twenty-five hundred! *About twenty-five hundred!* By G—d! you a regular officer, and come here to me and report *about* the number of men in your command. G—d d—n you, don't you know sir, you should furnish me the exact number?"

Davis—"General, I did'nt expect to get the guns now, and only wanted to learn if I could get them, and where, and having learned the exact number needed, would then draw them."

Nelson—pacing the floor in a rage—"About two thousand five hundred. By G—d, I suspend you from your command, and order you to report to General Wright, and I've a mind to put you under arrest. Leave my room, sir."

Davis—"I will not leave, General, until you give me an order."

Nelson—"The h—l you won't. By G—d I'll put

you under arrest, and send you out of the city under a provost guard. Leave my room, sir."

General Davis left the room, and in order to avoid an arrest, crossed over the river to Jeffersonville, where he remained until the next day, when he was joined by General Burbridge, who had also been relieved by Nelson for a trivial cause. General Davis came to Cincinnati with General Burbridge, and reported to General Wright, who ordered General Davis to return to Louisville, and report to General Buell, and General Burbridge to remain in Cincinnati. General Davis returned on Friday evening, and reported to General Buell.

Nothing further occurred until yesterday morning, when General Davis seeing General Nelson in the main hall of the Galt House, fronting the office, went up to Governor Morton and requested him to step up with him to General Nelson, and witness the conversation that might pass between Nelson and him. The Governor consented, and the two walked up to General Nelson, when the following took place:

General Davis—"Sir, you seemed to take advantage of your authority the other day."

General Nelson—sneeringly and placing his hand to his ear—"Speak louder, I don't hear very well."

Davis—in a louder tone—"You seemed to take advantage of your authority the other day."

Nelson—indignantly—"I don't know that I did, sir."

Davis—"You threatened to arrest and send me out of the State under a provost guard."

Nelson—striking Davis with the back of his hand twice in the face—"There, d—n you, take that."

Davis—retreating—"This is not the last of it; you will hear from me again."

General Nelson then turned to Governor Morton and said: "By G—d, did you come here also to insult me?"

Governor Morton—"No, sir; but I was requested to be present and listen to the conversation between you and General Davis."

General Nelson—violently to the bystanders—"Did you hear the d—d rascal insult me?" and then walked into the ladies' parlor.

In three minutes General Davis returned with a pistol he had borrowed of Captain Gibson, of Louisville, and walking toward the door that Nelson had passed through, he saw Nelson walking out of the parlor into the hall separating the main hall from the parlor. The two were face to face, and about ten yards apart, when General Davis drew his pistol and fired, the ball entering Nelson's heart, or in the immediate vicinity.

General Nelson threw up both hands and caught a gentleman near by around the neck, and exclaimed, "I'm shot." He then walked up the flight of stairs towards General Buell's room, but sank at the foot of the stairs, and was unable to proceed further. He was then conveyed to his room, and when laid on his bed, requested that Rev. Mr. Talbott, an Episcopal clergyman stopping at the house, might be sent to him at once. The reverend gentleman arrived in about five minutes.

Mr. Talbott found General Nelson extremely anxious as to his future welfare, and deeply penitent about the many sins he had committed. He knew he must die immediately, and requested the ordinance of baptism might be administered, which was done. The General then whispered: "It's all over," and died in fifteen minutes after he was conveyed to his room. His death was easy, the passing away of his spirit as though the General had fallen into a quiet sleep. His remains lay in state two days, and his funeral was witnessed by many of the Fifty-Ninth and other regiments.

General Davis immediately gave himself up to the military authorities to await a trial by court-martial.

This is the first case of the kind that has ever occurred in the American army, and its effect both North and South, will be startling. Nelson, although rough, tyrannical and insulting to General Davis, yet in a military point of view, General Davis was unjustifiable in shooting. Davis, however, has the sympathies of the people, both in Louisville and in the army, and would undoubtedly be pardoned by the President had a courtmatial found him guilty.

A brief review of General Davis' military career may not be uninteresting. He was born in Indiana, and is now about thirty-four years of age. He was married about six month since, and his wife is living fourteen miles back of Jeffersonville. He went to Mexico as a private, when only sixteen years of age; and on June 17, 1848, entered the regular army as Second Lieutenant of Artillery. He was with Major Anderson at Fort Sumter, and fired the first gun on the rebels at that celebrated engagement. His services, as officer of the guard, are well known to the public. After the surrender of the fort, he sailed in the Baltic for New York, and was ordered to Indianapolis as Mustering Officer, Quartermaster and Commissary. Remaining in this duty three months, he was appointed Colonel of the Twenty-Second Indiana Regiment, and was ordered to Jefferson City, Mo., to command that post with twelve thousand men under him. It was here he held important correspondence with General Fremont, upon the necessity of reinforcing Colonel Mulligan, at Lexington. He was ordered to report himself on the Potomac, with other regular officers. Arriving at St. Louis, General Halleck ordered him to report by letter and remain with him. Davis was then sent to Tipton, and there moved in junction with the force of General Curtis to Lebanon, Springfield and Pea Ridge. At the latter place, in the great battle, General Davis commanded the third or center division. After the battle, the officers of his division petitioned the President to appoint him Major General.

At Blackwater, Mo., General Davis captured one thousand three hundred prisoners, with two hundred and forty cavalry and three pieces of artillery. Among the number was Colonel Magoffin and three other Colonels, four Majors and a number of inferior officers.

The President forwarded a commission for a Brigadier General, and he was ordered to Corinth, at which place he arrived with his command two days before the evacuation. He continued with General Halleck until at Jacinto, Miss., he obtained twenty days leave to return home. He was unable to return and join his command, and thus he was thrown into Louisville.

General Nelson went from Kentucky into the navy as a Lieutenant, and with his movements and actions in the army in Kentucky, since the war broke out, every one is familiar. He was made a Brigadier General on the 16th of September, 1862, and afterwards promoted to the rank of Major General. He was formerly a resident of Maysville, and never was married. He has a large circle of relatives in the State, and a few residing in the East. He was also a relative of Mrs. Lincoln.

CHAPTER XXII.

After resting four days at Louisville, the regiment, on the morning of the 1st of October, received orders to pack up and be ready to move out at ten o'clock. The army was partially re-organized at Louisville, and the Fifty-Ninth Illinois, Twenty-Second Indiana, Seventy-Fifth Illinois and Seventy-Fourth Illinois regiments composed the Third Brigade of the Ninth Division of the army of the Ohio, with Colonel P. S. Post, of the Fifty-Ninth Illinois, commanding; and Brigadier General Jeff. C. Davis commanding the division. The command of the Fifty-Ninth now again devolved on the Lieutenant Colonel, C. H. Frederick. At ten o'clock the brigade moved out, and, passing through the city, took the Bardstown road.

It was now known that General Bragg, with thirty-five thousand men, was at Bardstown, Kentucky, and the supposition was that General Buell would meet him at that place, where a general engagement would be had.

Bardstown is thirty-five miles from Louisville and a forced march of twenty-four hours would bring the two armies together.

The old troops were all anxious to overtake the rebel army and give it battle. They had marched from one point to another until they had lost all patience, and would rather fight the enemy, two to one, than follow him any further. The new troops were also willing to encounter the foe if necessary—but would as soon have remained at Louisville, with their paper collars and black boots, and their nice light bread and butter. The first day or two after leaving the city these green soldiers looked upon the war-worn veterans as dirty, lousy fellows, unfit for associates to such nice clean gentlemen as they were. Two or three days march, however, began to reverse the feeling and by the time their appetite for hard tack and sow-belly had become of full growth they looked upon the old regiments with some degree of reverence and a considerable amount of awe. While they were dragging their sore and weary feet along, the old soldier marched with ease and martial bearing, and while these poor fellows were mincing and making wry faces at fat bacon and pilot bread, and dreaming of butter and baker's bread, the veterans were delighting over their good fare, and resting well o' nights. And the lice preferring new fields of enterprise, left their old haunts and established new quarters on these fresh troops.

Although two days easy marching would have taken the army to Bardstown, its advance did not arrive there until the fourth, and then only to find the town evacuated by the enemy. The Fifty-Ninth passed through Bardstown and encamped one mile east. Here the sick was selected from those able to march and sent back to hospital. Here, also, P. Sidney Post, commanding brigade, and Lieutenant Colonel Frederick, commanding regiment, remained behind, by order of the Surgeon, on account of ill health. The command of the regiment, in the absence of Frederick, devolved, of course, upon the Major, J. C. Winters.

It was now rumored that the enemy would give battle either at Danville or some selected position this side. The three succeeding days were therefore taken up in reconnoitering and slow marching. On the morning of the 8th cannonading was heard some distance to the left, and the command, of which the Fifty-Ninth formed a part, was advanced some two or three miles in the direction of Perryville. The cannonading continued with only short intervals during the day. The Ninth Division changed positions slightly during the day, but did not get within striking distance of the enemy until just before the dusk of the evening and only one brigade of this division *then* became engaged.

The enemy had met the left wing of our army early in the morning, and the battle had raged along the line towards the center until the whole left wing had become engaged, and now, about four o'clock, the right of the left wing was being rapidly forced back by an overwhelming concentration of the rebel forces.

To save his division from utter destruction, General McCook sent an urgent request that the Third Brigade of General Davis' division be immediately forwarded to the rescue. The Third Brigade is composed of the Fifty-Ninth Illinois, Twenty-Second Indiana, Seventy-Fourth and Seventy-Fifth Illinois. The Seventy-Fourth and Seventy-Fifth were new regiments, just from home. The distance to the point of danger was something less than a mile. It was now nearly sunset. Cheerfully the brigade marched out to meet the foe. The men had been held within hearing distance of the fearful carnage all day, with feelings akin to those of the chained lion when most eager for his prey.

Many were the inquiries, "Why are all these thousands of soldiers kept here idle all the day so near the battle-field?" "Why not move them to the assistance of our brave boys on the left?" The General in command alone stands responsible to his country and his God for a satisfactory answer to these inquiries.

Very many of those who witnessed the movement of the army at Perryville believe in their hearts that General Buell desired the destruction of his own army instead of that of Braxton Bragg's. The good generalship of his subordinates, and the bravery of the troops engaged, most gloriously defeated his designs.

It is impossible to give a description of the part the Third Brigade played in this dreadful tragedy.

The brigade was commanded by Colonel Goodin, of the Twenty-Second Indiana. The Colonel bravely conducted the regiments to the position assigned them, but before he could form them in battle array, the enemy opened fire with grape and cannister from their batteries, and poured volley after volley of musketry into his ranks. Nothing daunted, the brave men returned the fire with fatal effect for half an hour, each one loading and firing as rapidly as possible without order or system.

The enemy at this point had massed their forces for the purpose of turning the right flank of the left wing, which, if accomplished, would have placed it entirely at their mercy, and numbered at least ten to one of our brigade. It was useless to attempt to resist this mighty host, and the order was therefore given for each one to provide for his own safety. Major Winters, of the Fifty-Ninth, repeated the order the third time before the men ceased firing, and then they most reluctantly left the field. Fortunately the ground on which the brigade was halted by the proximity of the enemy was most favorable. Owing to the dusk of the evening and the favorable formation of the ground many of the rebel bullets overshot the mark. Those on horseback were in the most danger. The escape, however, of any of the brigade seems almost a miracle. The slaughter of the rebels in that half hour was dreadful. The idea of cutting off and capturing the left wing of the "Yankee army," as one of the wounded prisoners remarked the next morning, was driven from "Braxton's cranium." That night they evacuated the field, leaving their dead to show the execution of the Third Brigade in thinning their ranks during that short contest. The ground was literally covered with the dead and wounded of both sides. The loss to the Third was heavy, but to the rebels enormous. Every shot from the patriot guns must have taken effect.

The Fifty-Ninth, on going into the trap, numbered two hundred and ninety-one men, and on coming out brought off one hundred and eighty-three—leaving one hundred and eight on the field; twenty-three of whom were killed, sixty-two wounded, and twenty-three taken prisoners. Some of the other regiments lost more heavily. The wounded all lay on the field until next morning. The rebels holding the ground until daylight. As soon as it was ascertained that the enemy had retreated, the ambulances were sent out to gather up the wounded and convey them to hospital. The pen can convey no adequate conception of the scene presented on that small field that morning.

In the approach to the ground, the ambulances pass through a lane leading from some thick-timbered land to the mansion of the plantation on which the trap was set. Leaving the timber, a small open field on each side of the lane is passed, and then a thinly-wooded pasture-field to the left, and open fields on the right, extending to and surrounding the house. The appearance of the field now shows that the rebels were advancing en mass, through these open fields, from the mansion towards the thinly-wooded field to the left, when the Third Brigade was marched in, directly in front of them, to the wooded pasture-field. The distance from the house to this field was less than half a mile. Through the lower side of this field a small ravine passed, and from it the ground gradually ascended towards the mansion. The Third was marched down this ravine, and in easy range of the rebel muskets. The ravine was not deep enough to protect entirely from the rebel bullets, but the rising ground in front caused the enemy to overshoot, to a great extent. In this little woods-pasture lay the dead and wounded of the Third, with now and then a rebel in the midst, showing that our boys had fired as they fell back, and killed some of their pursuers. The grounds between this and the house, to the right and left, was strewn with dead rebels. More than five to one of those in the field, belonging to the Third, was here stretched out, in full possession of their deserved Southern rights.

The sixty-two wounded of the Fifty-Ninth were soon collected, and carefully transported to hospital, among whom was Adjutant Samuel West. Samuel West entered the service as a private, in Captain Hale's company (A.) He was appointed Sergeant-Major soon after the organization of the regiment, and, during the campaigns through Missouri and Arkansas, most satisfactorily performed the duties of that position. On the march he was daily seen with his knapsack on his back, keeping step with the men in the ranks, and in camp he was constantly engaged in doing his own legitimate business, as well as the principal part of that belonging to the commanding officer of the regiment. When **Adjutant P. Sidney Post** received his commission as Colonel of the regiment, West was promoted to the place of Adjutant. This position he has filled, with honor to himself and much benefit to the regiment, until now. At the battle of Pea Ridge, as Sergeant-Major, he gave that indication of bravery, and coolness in battle, which so clearly manifested itself at Perryville, while striving to preserve order and encourage the men to battle valiantly for their country. Very soon after coming in sight of the enemy, a ball hit him in the leg, above the knee, and soon another, and another, and yet another, and still another, which brought him from his horse, and he was carried from the field. Five times was the leaden messenger sent into his person, but, fortunately, at no vital point. Although so many times severely wounded, he eventually recovered, with the loss of only one eye. The loss was great, to be sure, but thankful, no doubt, was the Adjutant to escape with even so great a loss.

Another of the severely wounded was Captain Charles F. Adams, commanding Company I. Captain Adams was promoted from First Lieutenant, soon after the resignation of the former Captain of the Company, (Captain James A. Beach,) and, by his gentlemanly manners and kind treatment of his men, had become very much endeared to them. He was mortally wounded, and died in hospital, on the 15th day of October, 1862.

Company A lost one man killed—Francis W. Goff.

Company B lost its First Lieutenant—A. R. Johnson—than whom no one was more highly esteemed. He had always been a faithful soldier, and a good officer. His manners and habits were those of a gentleman and a christian.

The killed of Company C were Corporal F. C. Cherry, Henry Imel, William H. Blane, Thomas Loyd, James M. Jones, William H. Japaw. Of Company D, Thomas Abbott, Elias Walden. Company F: William H. Layman, Leander Reese, George W. Malatt. Company G: Sergeant William R. March, Harry M. Strickland James Cade and Joseph Geering, who died on the 11th from the effects of his wounds. Company K, Christian Assmus.

Doctor Hazlett, the Surgeon of the Regiment, was, also, numbered amongst the slain. He was shot through the neck while dressing the wound of a soldier. His remains were found the next morning, and through the instrumentality of Captain Snyder, of Company K, were respectably buried beneath the sheltering branches of an evergreen tree that stood close beside the spot where he was found. His boots had been stolen from his feet. A gold watch, and several hundred dollars in money, had been taken from his pockets. His hat, and a splendid case of instruments, were also gone. The Doctor rode a very fine horse, most splendidly caparisoned, and he, too, was gone.

In Doctor Hazlett the regiment had lost a very fine gentleman, and a scholar. He was not so universally respected by the men of the regiment as he, perhaps, deserved. His position was one requiring peculiar abilities, which, in many respects, the Doctor was deficient in. Surgical skill will secure a full reputation at the operating table, but something more is required to secure the entire approbation of a regiment of indiscriminating soldiers. His head was covered with hair silvered o'er, not with age, but naturally, and some gave him the epithet of "Tow-head." His prescriptions consisted largely in quinine, and hence the name of "Quinine" was frequently applied.

He, one time after a hard day's march, proposed to treat the regiment to a good "snort" of whisky. This was received with a hurrah by the men, but, on taking the "snort," it was so bitter with quinine that the wry faces along the line were universal.

Captain Clayton Hale, who was now acting Major, had his horse shot from under him while in advance of the regiment, transmitting orders to the men. He soon, however, procured another, and with it made his escape.

Colonel Goodin, commanding the brigade, was captured, and, with the other prisoners, taken to General Bragg's head-quarters, where they were paroled, and sent back into the Union lines.

The 9th was principally occupied in burying the dead and providing for the wounded. The regiment, however, moved about one mile farther to the right, and lay in that position until noon of the 10th, when it again moved some four miles in the opposite direction, going into camp near the point where the battle first commenced, on the morning of the 8th. Here were many indications of the severity of the contest. Dead rebels were everywhere met with, through the woods, as yet unburied. Two of them lay within twenty steps of the regiment for twenty-four hours after its arrival there, and would have rotted above ground had not some friends of theirs scattered dirt over them. Not that the Fifty-Ninth was unfeeling or inhuman, but it was not their business to kill, and then bury traitors. Close by was a small open field, in which were three hundred muskets, apparently thrown down by some regiment that had been camped there.

CHAPTER XXIII.

On the morning of the 12th, the regiment again moved out in pursuit of the enemy. Passing through Danville on the 13th, and through Lancaster on the 14th, it arrived in the neighborhood of Crab Orchard, on the evening of the 15th, and went into camp on the bank of Dix River, Ky., two miles from Crab Orchard, on the morning of the 16th, or rather the army went into bivouac, for the tents and camp equipage were yet in Louisville. An order, however, was immediately sent back to have them brought up. The distance marched since leaving Louisville, is one hundred and thirty miles. And here and thus ends Don Carlos Buell's campaign in Kentucky. A campaign which should have resulted in the capture or annihilation of the rebel hordes, but which will hereafter be regarded as one of the most miserable failures in the military history of the country. True, the State of Kentucky is now rid of the insolent, thieving foe, but this was not the task assigned the commander of the army of the Ohio. He was expected to utterly destroy them, and he had the men and the opportunities to do so; but instead, he permitted the enemy to fall upon, in force, and almost destroy a wing of his army, when fifty thousand men were in easy supporting distance; and then, as if to complete his work of imbecility or treachery, allowed them to escape, when their retreat might still have been cut off.

It is said that the army in Flanders swore terribly, and there is no doubt of that fact. Most armies do. But if any one had been fond of profanity, and wished to hear vigorous denunciations, in unmistakable Saxon, they should have heard the army of the Ohio, on the merits of the arch traitor, Don Carlos Buell.

The third great error of the war was now most clearly demonstrated—that of continuing Don Carlos in command, after his arrival at Louisville, Ky.

Here is an extract from a soldier's letter, written to his boy at home, after losing his summer's harvest by the excessive high waters of that season, showing in what the thoughts of the soldier frequently consist while idle in camp:

"DANVILLE, KY., October 22, 1862.

"DEAR SON:—For the first time since the 28th of September, I am sitting in a tent, writing. We came here yesterday, and are indebted to the report that some rebel cavalry are following us up pretty closely, for the purpose of picking up stragglers or capturing some of our train, for our leisure day. Our army is moving back to Lebanon, which is on the Louisville and Nashville railroad, and our brigade is the rear guard.

"We left Crab Orchard, Monday morning, and got this far, when we were halted, and two regiments, the Twenty-Second Indiana and Seventy-Fourth Illinois, were sent back to attend to the rebels. We will, perhaps, only remain here until these regiments return, and then move on.

"This is a beautiful day, and causes me to think of home. I would delight, above all things, to be with you this pleasant afternoon. I should like to look around with you, and see what you have left after your year's hard work. I know it is not much, but perhaps what you have is worth looking at. You have two or three nice 'shoats' in the pen, which you are feeding for your winter's meat. They are doing finely—will make fine, tender, juicy ham, such as we in the army are not accustomed to. Their spare-ribs will be most delicious, and the sausage meat you can get from them will repay you for the trouble of making it. Chickens you have, I see, in abundance—ah! yes, they are very nice. One fried now and then is not bad in a small family like yours, or even made into a pot-pie, is not hard to take—decidedly better than a dose of rheubarb. I see one there, now, that would do either for a fry or a stew—that one with the plump breast and yellow legs. Yes, chickens are a great help to a family, but an army has no use for chickens. The individual soldier sometimes finds use for them, as the people living along the line of march have learned to their sorrow.

"I see that you have a milch cow or two. Well, I reckon you make that which some people call butter, from the milk of the cow. Butter, if I remember rightly, is a yellow greasy substance which people sometimes spread on bread or hot biscuit, which, as they fancy, adds materially to their relish. I suppose it is quite necessary to those who have learned to use it, judging from the longing of the new recruits after it on leaving Louisville; but we in the army have no use for such stuff, and consequently a cow would be of no service to us, while alive, at any rate. If she had been starved a few weeks, and then skinned, we, perhaps, could make use of her bones for making soup, as we understand *that*. Ah, ha, you have one horse left too. Well, that's better than some folks I know of down here in Dixie. The less stock you have the less feed it takes, and the more time you have to spare for something else. And then there is another consolation about it—your taxes will not be so great next year. And then also you will not be called up o' nights to see if your horses haven't got loose in the stable and gone to kicking each other in the dark. I think it is a blessed thing to have nothing. Now, when we left Bowling Green, Kentucky, on our march from Nashville to Louisville, our wagons were all left behind, and all the knapsacks and trunks left with them. Our young officers had lots of fine clothes, etc., in their trunks, and our soldiers had pants, coats, etc., in their knapsacks, which were all left and consequently lost, and now they are lamenting their heavy losses. *I* had nothing of the sort. The clothes on my back—two shirts and two or three pair of socks—was all I had, and of course I brought them with me and lost nothing; consequently did'nt care a snap about the wagons, and now one little handkerchief will hold all my worldly goods, and I am as happy as—a fish on dry land. So I say, blessed be nothing."

On the morning of the 26th the brigade moved out for Lebanon; passing through Lebanon, it took the direct road for Bowling Green, where it arrived on the morning of the 4th of November. In the meantime General Rosecranz, succeeding Buell in command, had arrived at Bowling Green, and was personally inspecting and forwarding the different divisions on towards Nashville as fast as they arrived.

General Jeff. C. Davis, having been released from arrest, for shooting General Nelson, also arrived here and assumed command of his division.

Here, too, the Fifty-Ninth received an unlooked for acquisition, in the shape of an Assistant Surgeon from

Knoxville, Illinois. Charles Bunce reported himself for duty as a commissioned Surgeon of the Fifty-Ninth Regiment Illinois Volunteers, somewhat to the astonishment of the men, as no intimation of his appointment had ever reached them. It would naturally be supposed that the men of a regiment would be more deeply interested in the selection of a proper person to look after the health than any others, and in most regiments they have the selection of their own Surgeon, but in the Fifty-Ninth it seems to have been taken for granted that the men were mere automatoms, only fit to be looked after as a lot of mules should be in corral.

It is a universally admitted fact that many more men die in the army from other causes, than those produced by the shot and shell of the enemy. Some would fain believe that disease alone is chargeable with this fatality, but it is not so. A large majority of the fatal cases in the army are, *without a doubt*, produced by the malpractice of ignorant young men, who, through the influence of some personal friend, receive a commission as Surgeon. Very culpable is that man who recommends to the position of Surgeon a man entirely unfitted for the place, merely because he is a personal friend or relative. There are many young men who are now tampering with the lives of the noble soldier, whose qualifications are only such as they have acquired in attendance behind the counter of some one-horse drug store, or such as is obtained by taking care of some eminent doctor's horses. There is no other position in the army having so great a weight of responsibility attached as that of Surgeon, and there is no other position filled with so little regard to qualification as this one. It is to be hoped that more care may be bestowed by those in authority in ascertaining the qualifications of those sent to preserve the health and lives of the soldiers.

Leaving Bowling Green the regiment passes over the same road it had traversed about a month before, and arrives at Edgefield on the evening of the 7th of November, 1862. The only incident of note on the march was the burning, by the "Louisville Legion," of two large residences, from the windows of which they had been shot at while passing towards Nashville on their former visit, and the capturing of eleven prisoners, by our advanced skirmishers, on the morning of the 6th.

The distance from Crab Orchard to Nashville, via the route marched, is one hundred and fifty-six miles.

CHAPTER XXIV.

The morning of the 8th of November broke clear and frosty over the tired and sleepy soldiers of the army of the Cumberland. The town clock of Nashville failed to wake them at the proper time for revielle, and the fife and drum kept silence until the sun had sent his piercing rays into many a sleeper's face. Anon the drums begin to sound the signal for the morning roll call, and now the scene is changed. Men are seen in all directions creeping out from under blankets, wet with melting frost—some in full uniform, having slept all night in full dress; some half undressed, and some old veterans falling in for roll call with coat and pants both off. The custom in camp is to put on extra duty all who fail to answer at roll call.

Early in the forenoon, Colonel Frederick, who has regained his health and is now with the regiment, received orders to establish his regiment in camp. Colonel Frederick delighted in having order and neatness through his camping grounds, and consequently always superintended the pitching of tents and policing the camps himself.

The ground on which the tents were to be pitched, was a rolling piece of land, belonging to an old secesh, and delightfully situated for a camp. It was about half a mile from Edgefield, which is on the right bank of the Cumberland River, immediately opposite the city of Nashville, was well shaded by several large forest trees, and covered nicely by a good coating of blue grass. The river affords a good supply of water, and several springs are close at hand.

The tents are pitched something after military regulations, but not exact. The Colonel selecting the position of the tents to suit his fancy. The soldiers' tents are pitched in line by companies. First is company A, at the right of the regiment; next in order is company B; next, C, and so on down to company K, on the left. The company tents are set in line, one behind the other, with a space of thirty feet between the companies. In front of these are the tents of the commanders of companies; each Captain thirty feet in front of his company. Thirty feet in front of these again, are the tents of the field and staff officers. When regularly pitched, and with clean white tents, the appearance is quite pretty. Each regiment has its own separate grounds, in connection with its own brigade. A brigade consists of four regiments and a battery, and covers several acres.

Now, then, what is the daily occupation of the inhabitants of these tents? Persons not in the secret might suppose that there was nothing to do but eat and sleep, and amusement generally. But not so. In the morning at four or five o'clock, reveille is sounded by the drums and fife. This notifies the sleeper that he must get up and answer to his name at roll call. The Orderly Sergeant calls the roll, in the presence of some one of the commissioned officers of the company. Fires are now kindled, and each one prepares his own breakfast. After breakfast the "sick call" is sounded. The Orderly Sergeant then reports all the sick men in his company to the Doctor. Sometimes there are twenty or thirty brought to him for examination and medicine.

Those who are really sick, the Doctor excuses from doing any duty that day, so that he may lay around at his leisure and get well; or, perhaps, he is retained at the hospital, where he can be nursed and have medicine given him.

At eight o'clock comes guard mounting—that is, placing guards around the camp, so that soldiers can't leave camp without a pass or written permit from the Colonel. These guards are stationed all around camp at certain intervals, and must continually walk back and forth from one station to the other, so that they can see any one who tries to pass out. One man walks two hours, then another relieves him. This set of guards remain on duty for twenty-four hours. New guards are mounted every morning. After guard mounting, extra-duty men are usually set to work sweeping the grounds. By the time this is done, dinner is to be prepared. In the afternoon, the men are taken out on battalion drill, usually from two o'clock until four. Then supper. After this comes dress parade. At sundown the drums beat retreat. At eight, tattoo; and at nine, all becomes quiet—the day's work is done. This is the daily employment of the soldier in camp. But there is some other work that has to be attended to, such as going out on picket, for instance, one company or a part of a company, is sent out a mile or two from camp, to stay for twenty-four hours, so that an enemy may not make a surprise on the camp. There is, also, other work to be done, such as drawing rations, getting wood, washing clothes, &c. The soldier's life is not an idle one.

While the regiment lay at Florence, Ala., several contrabands came to camp and engaged themselves as servants to the officers; amongst them were two females.

One of these soon donned the habiliments of a soldier. In this garb she marched with the regiment until now. On the evening of the 7th, when coming into camp, she incidentally passed through the yard of the planter, close to the chicken roost. The guard stationed there supposed that she was after some of the feathered tribe, and ordered her to halt. Not supposing the order addressed to her, she paid no attention to it, and was passing on, when the guard fired, shooting her in the "seat of honor." The guard did not suspect he was shooting a woman; but supposed her to be some thieving buck negro. She was taken to camp, and now Dr. Bunce had the opportunity of performing his first surgical operation. The wound was merely a flesh wound, and the most difficult part of the operation was the examination, in the presence of several unfeeling witnesses. The Doctor soon applied the dressing—very neatly, considering the circumstances—and then left nature to perform the healing.

On the 30th the Division crossed the river, and pitched tents again, south of Nashville. An extract from the author's diary, of the 5th December, says:

"We are still in camp, four miles south of town, and nothing, as yet, indicating a move. Our pleasant weather has gone, 'glimmering among the dream of things that were,' and now we are wrapping our blankets and over-coats around us to keep out the chilling north winds, and to protect us from the driving snow. To-day the snow has been filling the air with its downy flakes, and covering the earth and trees with a beautiful garment of white. This is the second time since last winter that the earth has been clothed in a symbol of purity. There are, however, but slight indications of its continuing in that gait long, for even now rents are perceivable, through which its nakedness is manifest. The warmth of the ground is too great for the snow's frail fabric, and not long can it resist the heating influence. Perhaps by to-morrow's eve it will have returned to its native element, and disappeared. Snow in the Northern States, when the ground is hard frozen, is a great benefit to the farmer in protecting his small grain; but in the South, where it falls one day and disappears the next, is of little profit, yet it is not without its use, as there is no providential occurrence without some good result."

The diary continues:

"6th—Another morning has dawned, bright and cold. After the snow-storm, yesterday, the clouds passed away, and the night set in with a clear sky and brilliant moon, and stars innumerable. This morning the snow is crackling under feet, and glistening in the sun-beams splendidly. It is the coldest morning of the season, but old Sol will soon warm the atmosphere to a pleasant temperature. The woodman's axe is ringing merrily in all directions. The soldiers are busy cutting down the trees for wood, that they may have warm fires to stay by these cold mornings. In a very short time this noble grove will be all destroyed. 'Woodman, spare that tree,' is not the motto here. The delight of the soldier seems to be, to lay the monarch of the forest low, in this secesh country.

"One old lady, on whose premises we camped one day, exclaimed:

"'Good Lord! are they going to cut *all* our trees?'

"Her husband was in the rebel army, and her trees were not spared. Before the army left, stumps alone remained to tell the fate of that splendid grove—a grove, of which the old lady had been proud for many years, and with which she was very loth to part. Her children, and her grand children, had delighted her old heart many times with their childish gambols, under those noble shade-trees; but, alas, and alack! they are gone now; and the grass that is now so green and bright will be all withered and browned by the scorching rays of the sun. The next generation will have to play in the sunshine, or seek some other grove in which to sport. It will not be so bad for the little woolly-headed darkies, as their complexion is but little affected by the tanning influence of the sun; but the fair skin of the white children will suffer.

"7th December, 1862—This is a cold, bright Sabbath. Winter is here in earnest. We in camp are well prepared for cold weather. The boys have plenty of good, warm clothing, and blankets, over-coats and tents, and, if they suffer, it will be because they will not get wood for their fires.

"December 8th—The snow has all disappeared, but the weather is still cold. The paymaster has been paying off a part of the regiment to-day. Company F fails to get pay because of having no pay rolls. Captain Currie, who has lately been transferred to the gun-boat service, left the regiment a few days ago, and carried the rolls along with him, very much to the inconvenience of the company. Lieutenant Maddox is now in command of the company.

"December 9th—It yet continues most charming winter weather. In fact it more resembles early spring than winter.

"Something is now going on four or five miles from here. What it is we do not know; but the reports from secesh cannon indicate a skirmish with the enemy, some foraging party being resisted in their depredations. The regiment is going out on a scout of a few hours, and will ascertain, perhaps, what that cannonading means. I think it is quite time that Rosecranz was doing something. One month has passed since we arrived at Nashville, and no advance has yet been made. Why remain idle so long? The men are all anxious to move forward, and do something towards terminating the war. Better die fighting the enemy than linger out a miserable existence in camp.

"8 o'clock—The regiment has just returned to camp, without learning anything of the cannonading. They bring no spoils of victory, except one or two contraband hogs, and a few chickens.

"December 10th—Reveille sounded in the old camp this morning at two o'clock, and at five we moved out on the march. Our course was taken due east from camp, as could be known by the redness of the horizon, indicating the point at which the 'God of day' would first make his appearance. The morning was cool and bracing, and the boys put out with a will, being also encouraged by a prospect of a fight with the enemy, as it was rumored that that was the object of the march. The march continued about five miles, and terminated by our going into camp here. We are, perhaps, a little nearer the enemy than we were this morning, but have only changed our position in relation to Nashville. We are now more directly between Nashville and Murfreesboro'—four miles from the former, and twenty-six from the latter—about two miles west of the pike leading to Murfreesboro'. This State, as well as Kentucky, is abundantly supplied with macadamized roads. Stone is easily procured, and has been unsparingly used for road purposes.

"It is now about four o'clock on the morning of the

11th of December. 'Early to bed and early to rise' is an example set by all who have ever made any great progress in the world, and this morning I have followed it. Early rising is pretty generally practiced in the army, especially by the privates; the officers, having attained to all they desire, sleep till surfeited.

"This is a lovely morning, just such an one as would suit me at home. Oh, how much I would enjoy home this morning! The christian, who has resigned his claim to all earthly things, and transferred his treasures to the 'better land,' alone can tell the feelings of a soldier when he *indulges* in the thoughts of home. Home, to the soldier, is as the treasure-house above to the christian, for where the treasures are there will the heart be also. 'Home, sweet home, there is no place like home.' 'Oh, dark is how my heart grows weary, far from my good old home.' Shall I never more behold it? Never again look upon the bright and cheerful faces of those I left behind me there? Yes, I fancy that I shall, but the time seems long—seems very long.

"Well, I have just returned from a walk I have been taking, out beyond the camp, and there the birds bid me be of good cheer. They sang, 'When the spring time comes,' you may with us go back to your northern home, and we'll spend the summer together there. I blessed the little songsters, and came back to camp more resigned and cheerful. *Now* the day is numbered amongst those that were before the flood, and a 'wee bit' candle is all the light I have to see by.

"About half a mile from camp is a large cane brake, or cane thicket. The cane stands so thick on the ground that a hare could not pass between them, only in places where they had been cut or broken down. They are from fifteen to twenty feet in length; they are now in thick foliage; the leaves are as green as in the summer time; it is quite cheering to look at them. The little birds come from miles away to sleep among the thick leaves; it is so much warmer for them than on the branches of the big leafless trees of the forest. Here the cold wind or the sharp frost can not penetrate; but the innocent little creatures had better run the risk of being frozen than seek shelter here at this time, for every night hundreds of them are sacrificed to the rapacity of the ruthless soldier. The boys take candles and torches, and by dazzling their eyes with the bright light, pick them from their perches without difficulty, or knock them off with sticks do they try to escape. The birds are principally the red-breasted robbin, but there are other smaller ones of different kinds. Pot-pie is a commonn dish in camp now.

"December 12th—The mail comes regularly to camp now, bringing letters from the dear ones at home. Good, kind, cheering letters some of them are too. I just had the pleasure of reading one from a good old mother in Illinois to her noble boy in the army. Such loving, cheering words—such good advice. The boy's heart was softened, ennobled, elevated. There is no danger of his becoming wicked so long as that kind mother continues her controlling influence over him. Would that there were more such mothers in Illinois! If there were there would be much less wickedness manifested in the army of the Cumberland. No one can estimate the restraining influence of an affectionate letter from a beloved mother, or a kind friend, to the young soldier. I fancy that I can go through our regiment and point out every young man who has a good family at home, or a pious loving mother who devotes a portion of her time in writing to her soldier boy in the army.

Richly will she be rewarded for labor thus spent. The soldier is constantly exposed to peculiar temptations, and needs all the restraining influences that can be thrown around him, and there can be none more restraining than the admonitions of an absent, loving mother.

"December 22d—The weather continues most delightful. We are under marching orders. The tents are all struck and loaded in the wagons. The sick have all been sent back to Nashville to remain in hospital until their health becomes restored, or they are transported to that bourne from whence no traveler returns.

"Mason Campbell, of Company B, was under treatment at the regimental hospital three days before being sent to Nashville. The most energetic treatment was pursued in his case—about five grains of calomel being given him every three hours for three days, making, in all, one hundred and twenty grains, and no motion from the bowels during the time; with all this he was sent to Nashville and died.

"December 25—Here we are in camp again. After loading our traps in the wagons we lay around promiscuously until yesterday noon, when we marched about five miles towards Nolensville, right about faced, and marched back again to the very spot we started from. "Strategy, my boy!"

"Occasional reports from artillery have been heard out in front to-day, and I shouldn't wonder if they were the harbingers of a battle shortly to take place.

"One of the boys deserted from the regiment last night, and it is supposed he has gone over to the rebels. He was tied up yesterday for leaving camp without first getting a pass. He slipped the guards and visited Nashville, where he remained all night. When he came back he was arrested by the Captain of his company and tied by both hands to the lower limbs of a tree, where he was kept some two hours or more. This morning he is missing. There are various ways of punishing men in the army. Some are tied up, either with their arms encircling the trunk of a large tree, or with their hands high above their heads. Some are made to pack rails on their shoulder with a guard following them, for two or three hours at a time.

"One young man was paraded through camp one day with both hands tied fast to a single-tree, hitched behind a mule; a man was riding the mule; two guards with fixed bayonets marching beside the captive, and the fife and drum beating the rogues march behind.

"Sometimes the punishment consists in having a board strapped to the back, with large letters in chalk, stating the offense, and being marched around through camp.

"In some cases it seems to be necessary not only to bind the hands but to tie the tongue also. This is done by forcing some substance into the mouth so as to keep the jaws separated. The practice of this sort of punishment by one of the officers gave him the name of 'Buck and Gag.'"

CHAPTER XXV.

On the morning of the 27th, every thing being in readiness, the division moved out, taking the direction of Nolinsville, which is nine miles from camp. The day was not so pleasant as was desirable, but the men were willing to march, and did not mind the rain and mud to be encountered.

Lieut. Colonel Frederick started out with the regiment in the morning, but having poor health, soon fell back to an ambulance and returned to Nashville. Major Winters was at home, on leave of absence, and Captain Hale, the ranking Captain in the regiment, was also absent. The command, therefore, fell to the lot of Captain Paine, of company B. Captain Paine was a strict disciplinarian, and commanded one of the best drilled companies in the regiment. His strict discipline and peculiar way of punishing his men, had procured for him the name of "Buck and Gag." Captain James M. Stookey, being the next ranking Captain assumed the position of Major. By this arrangement, company B was left to the command of First Lieutenant J. R. Johnson, and company E, to the command of Lieutenant Goodin.

Soon after leaving camp, the Fifty-Ninth was sent in advance as skirmishers. They soon came across the rebel pickets and began skirmishing. As the Fifty-Ninth advanced, the rebels in front of them fell back to the town of Nolensville, where it seems they intended to more severely contest the ground. Here they had a battery planted, and threw several shells at our men before they could get one in position to reply. As soon, however, as a shot or two was fired from a twelve pounder, placed in range, the rebels withdrew on double quick, and the Fifty-Ninth took possession of the town. As the regiment was advancing across an open common, between the woods and town, a volley was fired at one of the companies from the windows of a large frame house, in front of them, without doing any injury. Colonel Pease, of General Davis' staff, saw the shooting, and being close to one of our guns, ordered the cannoneer to plant a shell into the house. This gun had been instrumental in silencing the rebel battery, and was within good range of the house. The first shell exploded within one of the upper rooms, doing wonderful execution among the furniture and tearing the plastering and casing into a thousand fragments. This brought the rebs to light, and a volley from the company sent them howling to the woods. The second shell passed through the hen house, scattering chickens and feathers in all directions, and continuing on its course, burst in the rear of the fleeing rebels. The town was now in possession of the Fifty-Ninth, but to the right heavy skirmishing continued, and the regiment passed on in that direction. Heavy skirmishing continued until the enemy were driven to the opposite side of "Big Gap," about four miles south of Nolensville. Darkness now prevented any further pursuit, and the army went into bivouac. The loss in the division was light, the Fifty-Ninth not having a man hurt. Several of the enemy were killed and a few taken prisoners.

Colonel Pease, while setting on his horse, directing

the cannoneer, was hit on the leg by a minnie ball, which passed through his pants, just creasing the flesh. "That's pretty close," remarked the Colonel, and continued his directions without any further notice of the flying missiles.

The regiment here lost another man by desertion, or rather gained the room and rations of a worthless, thieving Frenchman. He was a member of company G, and had frequently offended by disobeying orders in regard to straggling, particularly in times of danger. There are a few men in all regiments who, whenever there is a prospect of a fight "play off" either by feigning sickness, or by slipping from the ranks on some trivial pretence, and dropping to the rear, there to remain until the danger is all over. This fellow of a Frenchman, had practiced this habitually, and now the Captain determined to punish him. This he did by tying him up. In a short time thereafter, the fellow managed to loosen the cords that bound him and make his escape. Pursuit was immediately made and an exciting chase resulted in the defeat of the pursuers. It is supposed the fellow fled to the rebel lines, and it is to be hoped that all sneaks who will fall back to the rear, to places of safety, when their friends and companions in arms are in danger, will follow his example, and cast their lot with traitors.

The morning of the 27th was so murky, that an enemy could not be seen at any distance, and consequently the troops did not move until the fog had disappeared in rain drops. About nine o'clock, the skirmishers were advanced and continued moving forward until evening, without meeting with any serious resistance. The Fifty-Ninth followed in regular marching order for six or eight miles, and went into bivouac.

The 28th being Sunday, the army lay in camp all day. General Rosecranz was religiously opposed to moving his army on the Sabbath, unless unavoidable. All honor and praise to him for setting such a noble example. Success will ever attend the General who pays due respect to the command, "Remember the Sabbath day to keep it holy."

This morning the Acting Adjutant, Hale Phillips—Adjutant West being on Colonel Post's brigade staff—and the Commissary Sergeant, Thomas J. Melvin, obtained permission to return to Nashville on business. On their way they overtook the train a few miles from Nashville. With the train was Captain Clayton Hale and Lieutenant Fred. Brasher, Quartermaster; the former returning to the regiment from a leave of absence, and the latter in charge of the train. Very soon after the Adjutant and Commissary arrived at the train, and before they had dismounted from their horses they were surrounded by a large squad of rebel cavalry and all taken prisoners. Resistance was useless, as there was no guard with the train, and consequently they surrendered without an effort to escape. They were treated very kindly by their captors—paroled and allowed to proceed to Nashville. From Nashville they visited their homes, and had a good time of it generally, until they were exchanged.

On Monday morning, December 29th, the army was again put in motion. General Davis, taking the advance of General McCook's corps, with his division, turned from the Nolensville pike, in an easterly direction, towards Murfreesboro'. The writer was fortunate enough to witness the passing of this corps, as it proceeded to the lane at which it left the pike. First came General Jeff. C. Davis and staff, immediately followed by a body guard of one company of cavalry. Next followed Colonel P. Sidney Post, commanding brigade, with his staff, and then the four regiments of his brigade, closely followed by a six gun battery. Then followed the other brigades in the same order. While the column was passing, General McCook and staff came dashing by in magnificent style. They came, they were seen, and they were gone. General McCook is a good commander, but like most of his rank, he prides himself on *being* General McCook. While looking at this well appointed corps, the heart swelled with emotions of pride, to think that there were so many noble-hearted men willing and eager to meet in deadly contest the enemy who were attempting to destroy their country.

The 29th and 30th were spent in reconnoitering and skirmishing with the enemy, General Davis' Division terminating its movements by getting into position Tuesday evening, on the left of McCook's command, near Wilkerson's Creek. The Fifty-Ninth Illinois Regiment occupied the left of Colonel P. Sidney Post's brigade, and the extreme left of the right wing of the army. The enemy had fallen back to their chosen position, about two miles from Murfreesboro', and the Fifty-Ninth Illinois lay on the ground all Tuesday night, within five hundred yards of their line of battle The night was quite cold, and the ground saturated with water. Without blankets or fires, the men shivered through the night. Company G, commanded by Captain Starkey, was stationed to the right of the regiment, and somewhat in advance, as picket-guard. This continued the position of the regiment until the rebels made the attack, Wednesday morning.

General Rosecranz marched from Nashville, with

forty-five thousand men, and one hundred and two pieces of artillery, and skirmished all the way to the battle field, the enemy resisting bitterly. The whole of Tuesday was spent in reconnoitering. The enemy was found strongly posted, with artillery, in a bend of Stone River, his flanks resting on the west side of Murfreesboro'.

The center also had the advantage of high ground with a dense growth of cedar masking them completelly. Their position gave them the advantage of a cross fire, and General McCook's Corps closed in their left on Wilkerson's Creek. Negley, of Thomas' Corps, worked, with great difficulty, to the front of the rebel center. Rousseau's Division was in reserve. Crittenden's Corps was posted on the comparatively clear ground on the left, Palmer's and Van Cleve's Divisions in front, in the woods, and held in reserve.

A battle was expected all day Tuesday, but the enemy merely skirmished and threw a few shells, one of which killed Orderly McDonald, of the Fourth United States Cavalry, not ten feet from General Rosecranz. That afternoon the Anderson Pennsylvania Cavalry, on McCook's flank, was drawn into an ambuscade, and its two Majors (Rosengarten and Ward) were killed.

Crittenden's Corps lost four killed and two wounded that day, including Adjutant Elliott, of the Fifty-Seventh Indiana, severely wounded. McCook's loss was about fifty. The same day the rebel cavalry made a dash on our rear, at Lavergne, burned a few wagons, and captured thirty-five prisoners. That night dispositions were made to attack the enemy in the morning. After dark the enemy were reported massing upon McCook, obviously to strike our right wing. This corresponded with the wishes of General Rosecranz, who

(13)

instructed General McCook to hold him in check stubbornly, while the left wing should be thrown into Murfreesboro', behind the enemy.

At daybreak, of the last day of December, everything appeared working well. Battle had opened on our right, and our left wing was on hand at seven o'clock. Ominous sounds indicated that the fire was approaching on the right. Aides were dispatched for information, and found the forests full of flying negroes, with some straggling soldiers, who reported whole regiments falling back rapidly. Meantime one of McCook's aides announced to General Rosecranz that General Johnson had permitted the three batteries of his division to be captured by a sudden attack of the enemy, and that that fact had somewhat demoralized the troops. This was obvious. The brave General Sill, one of our best officers, was killed, General Kirk severely wounded, and General Willich killed or missing, besides other valuable officers. General Rosecranz sent word, pressing General McCook to hold the front, and he would help him. It would all work right. He now galloped to the front of Crittenden's left, with his Staff, to order the line of battle, when the enemy opened a full battery and emptied two saddles of the escort. Van Cleve's Division was sent to the right, Colonel Beatty's Brigade in front. The fire continued to approach on the right with alarming rapidity, extending to the center, and it was clear that the right was doubling upon the left. The enemy had compelled us to make a complete change of front on that wing, and were pressing the center.

General Rosecranz, with splendid daring, dashed into the fire, and sent his Staff along the lines, started Beatty's Brigade forward, some six batteries opened, and sustained a magnificent fire. Directly a tremendous shout was raised along the whole line. The enemy began to fall back rapidly. The General himself urged the troops forward. The rebels, thoroughly punished, were driven back fully a mile. The same splendid bravery was displayed in the center, and the whole line advanced. Meantime the enemy made formidable demonstrations on our left, while they prepared for another onslaught on our right. Meantime orders had been issued to move our left upon the enemy. Before they had time to execute it, they burst upon our center with awful fury, and it began to break.

Rousseau's Divisions were carried into the breach magnificently by their glorious leader, and the enemy again retreated hastily into the dense cedar thickets. Again they essayed our right, and again were driven back. This time the number of our stragglers was formidable, and the prospect was discouraging, but there was no panic. The General, confident of success, continued to visit every part of the field, and, with the aid of Thomas, McCook, Crittenden Rousseau, Negley and Wood, the tide of battle was again turned.

Early in the day we were seriously embarrassed by the enterprise of rebel cavalry, who made some serious dashes upon some of McCook's ammunition and subsistence trains, capturing a number of wagons, and artillery ammunition was alarmingly scarce. At one time it was announced that not a single wagon-load of it could be found. Some of our batteries were quiet, on that account. This misfortune was caused by the capture of McCook's trains. About two o'clock the battle had shifted again, from right to left, the rebels discovering the impossibility of succeeding in their main design, and suddenly massed his forces on the left, crossing the river, or moving under high bluffs, from his right, and for about two hours the fight raged with unremitting fury. The advantage was with the enemy for a considerable length of time, when they were checked by our murderous fire, of both musketry and artillery. The scene at this point was magnificent and terrible. The whole battle was in full view, the enemy deploying right and left, bringing up their batteries in fine style, our own vomiting smoke and missiles upon them with awful fury, and our gallant fellows moving to the front with unflinching courage, or lying flat upon their faces to escape the rebel fire, until the moment for action. There was not a place on the field that did not give men a satisfactory idea of the manner of hot fire, solid shot, shell and minnie balls, which rattled around like hail. Rosecranz himself was incessantly exposed—it is wonderful that he escaped. His Chief of Staff (noble Lieutenant-Colonel Garesche) had his head taken off by a round shot, and the blood spattered the General and some of the Staff. Lieutenant Lyman Kirk, just behind him, was lifted clear out of his saddle by a bullet, which shattered his left arm. Three Orderlies, and the gallant Sergeant Richmond, of the Fourth United States Cavalry, were killed within a few feet of him, and five or six horses in the staff and escort were struck.

Between four and five o'clock the enemy, apparently exhausted by his rapid and incessant assault, took up a position not assailable without abundant artillery, and the fire on both sides slackened, and finally ceased at dark, the battle having raged eleven hours.

The loss of life on our side is considerable. The field is comparatively limited. The whole casualty list that day, excluding captures, did not exceed, perhaps, one thousand and five hundred, of whom not more than one-fourth were killed. This is attributed to the care taken to make our men lie down. The enemy's loss must have been more severe. But among our losses we mourn such noble souls as General Sill, General August Willich, Colonel Garesche, Colonel Minor Millikin, First Ohio Cavalry; Colonel Hawkins, Thirteenth Ohio; Colonel McKee, Third Kentucky; Colonel Gorman, Fifteenth Kentucky; Colonel Kell, Second Ohio; Lieutenant-Colonel Shepherd, Eighteenth Regulars; Major Carpenter, Nineteenth Regulars; Captain Edgarton, First Ohio Battery, and his two Lieutenants, and many more.

When the battle closed, the enemy occupied ground which was ours in the morning, and the advantage theirs. Their object in attacking was to cut us off from Nashville; they almost succeeded. They had played their old game. If McCook's corps had held more firmly against Hardee's corps and Cheatham's, when he fought, Rosecranz's plan of battle would have succeeded. At dark they had a heavy force on our right, leading to the belief that they intended to pursue. Their cavalry, meantime, was excessively troublesome, cutting deeply into our train behind us, and we had not cavalry enough to protect ourselves. The Fourth Regulars made one splendid dash at them, capturing sixty-seven and releasing five hundred prisoners they had taken from us. The enemy took a large number.

"General Rosecranz determined to begin the attack this morning and opened furiously with out left at dawn. The enemy, however, would not retire from our right, and the battle worked that way. At eleven o'clock matters were not flattering on either side. At twelve o'clock our artillery, new supplies of ammunition having arrived, was massed, and a terrible fire opened. The enemy began to give way, General Thomas pressing on their center, and Crittenden advancing on their left. The battle was more severe at that hour than it had been, and the result was yet doubtful. Both sides were uneasy, but determined. General Rosecranz feels its importance fully. If he is defeated it will be badly, because he will fight as long as he has a brigade. If he is victorious, the enemy will be destroyed. At this hour we are apprehensive. Some of our troops behaved badly, but most of them were heroes. The enemy seem to number as many as we, and perhaps more. General Joe Johnson and General Braxton Bragg are in command." Thus writes a correspondent of the Cincinnati Commercial.

When the enemy surprised General Johnson, the Fifty-Ninth Illinois was under arms and ready for the conflict. Had the attack been made on General Davis instead of Johnson the ground would have been held and the inglorious stampede of the right wing prevented. The attack was made at the only point in the Union lines where the rebels would not have met with a warm reception. Some of the boys were captured while at the Springs after water; some at their fires while cooking, and some of the artillery-men were surprised while watering their horses.

The attack was manfully resisted in front of the Fifty-Ninth Illinois until Johnson's Division had doubled back in confusion on Davis, and the enemy was forcing Davis' right so as to threaten the rear of Post's Brigade, when Colonel Post ordered a retreat. Reluctantly and in good order the regiment moved back, occasionally throwing a volley into the ranks of the pursuing enemy, which held them in check until General Rousseau's command came to the rescue. On its retreat it passed the point where our brigade battery had been in position. One gun of the battery had been left behind still in position, for the want of horses to pull it off the field, some of these having been killed. The men, by permission, left the ranks and soon run it out of danger of falling into the hands of the enemy. As soon as reinforcements arrived the Fifty-Ninth ceased its retreat and advanced again upon the enemy. They were driven back and the regiment went into bivouac north of the Murfreesboro' and Nashville Pike. Of all the regiments belonging to Johnson or Davis' divisions the Fifty-Ninth came off the field with the most men and in the best order.

James A. Howser, Company F, Sergeant John J. Hatham and Andrew J. Watts, Company D, James H. Sheets, Company C, Patrick Reynolds, Company II, Jas. R. Dennis, Company B, Sergeant Alfred B. Barber and Corporal Reuben Cummins, Company G, and Thos. I. Hopper, Company A, were left on the field killed. Jefferson Slusser and James Slusser were left on the field wounded, and fell into the hands of the rebels. They were taken to Murfreesboro', and kept there until retaken by our forces on the evacuation of the town.

On the 1st day of January, 1863, the regiment advanced to Stone River to within two miles of Murfreesboro', and General Davis being ordered to charge across and dislodge some of the enemy who were on the opposite side, the Fifty-Ninth waded the stream on double-quick, charged up the bank and took possession of the ground, the rebels retreating before their glittering bayonets without resistance. Here they lay under fire, and returning shot for shot until after dark, when they silently withdrew, crossing back to their old position.

The battle continuing through the 2d and 3d days of January; the regiment was constantly kept under arms, frequently changing position so as to always be in front of the enemy.

During the stampede on Wednesday the rebel cavalry broke through our lines and made a dash on the train. The hospital wagon of the Fifty-Ninth Regiment was halted by one of the Texan Rangers, and the driver was ordered to drive his team off in an opposite direction. "Certainly, certainly," said the driver, but in the meantime made his calculations, and sprang from the wagon on the other side. Some fleeing soldier had thrown away his loaded musket; this fortunately was seen by Foster—the driver's name was Albert Foster—who picked it up. Passing rapidly to the rear and around his wagon he shot the rebel from his horse, mounted it and joined our cavalry, which was now charging back on the greazy scoundrels, and assisted in driving them to the woods. After chasing them until pursuit was useless he returned to his team with his spoils of victory. The horse was a valuable one, and was well equipped with a good saddle and bridle, a pair of pistols in the holsters, and saddle-bags containing some clothing and corn bread. A few more such heroic drivers would save many a government wagon from the torch of the guerrilla.

The rebels retreated from Murfreesboro' on the night of the 3d, and on the 4th General Rosecranz established his headquarters there. The army moved on through town and went into camp two or three miles below. The trains were soon ordered up with tents and all necessary camp equipage, and in a few days the troops were comfortably resting from the excessive toil and exposure of the last two weeks' campaign. Eight days constant exposure without rest or sleep had tried the muscle and nerve of the brave men of the army to the extent, almost, of endurance. Nobly had they endured the hardships, and now they are entitled to all the comforts that is possible to be provided. They had driven the rebels from their comfortable winter quarters at Murfreesboro', and had made the prospect for a termination of the war much more flattering than when lying idly in camp at Nashville, and they were satisfied. Their hardships were soon forgotten, and in a very few days they would have been willing to have made another advance.

CHAPTER XXVI.

The Fifty-Ninth pitched tents to the right of the pike leading from Murfreesboro' to Shelbyville, three miles south of town. Stone River ran a short distance from camp on the right, and in front lay the large plantation of ex-senator Bell, recent candidate for Vice President of the United States, but now a traitor.

The splendid mansion of this arch traitor is now occupied by General Johnson, of the Union Army. The owner of this plantation fled with the rebel army on its retreat from the battle of Stone River, and General Johnson took possession and encamped his division on the premises the day following. The house is most delightfully situated on an elevated spot overlooking the whole plantation, and near the banks of Stone River. From the portico in front of the mansion, may be seen the pure, blue waters of the river, as it winds its tortuous course along its rock-bound channel, for two miles above and below. The negro cabins, and the slaves at work any where on the plantation, can be seen from the piazza, or could have been a few days ago; but now the white tents of the soldier has taken the place of the slave at his work.

The Fifty-Ninth was not allowed to enjoy a lengthy repose in camp, but was soon sent with a part of the division to reinforce the command at Franklin, Tenn., thirty miles west of Murfreesboro'. Leaving all but such things as they could carry in their knapsacks, they reached Franklin the second day after leaving camp. Here they lay in bivouac about ten days. They then returned to camp, bringing with them three or four prisoners and a few extra horses. The three prisoners and three horses were captured by two of our boys, Wm. Ebling and Samuel Wambroth; the one the hospital nurse, and the other a cook; being both mounted on extra horses, were a short distance from the road, when they saw three rebel horsemen riding across an open field towards a house in the distance. These two boys put spurs to their horses and made pursuit. On coming within hailing distance they shouted to the rebs to halt, which they did, surrendering themselves prisoners of war. The boys, proud of their capture, marched them off to General Davis, and they were handed over to the provost guard.

This same William Ebling, while scouting over the battle ground of Stone River the day after the battle terminated, came across a citizen dressed in butternut clothing, and supposing him to be a rebel, arrested him. Ebling had just before passed a sutler establishment and bought a bottle of whisky. Although he was death on rebels, he freely shared his whisky with his prisoner, and when he presented his captive to General Davis, they were both pretty tight. The man was a good Union man, and was hunting over the field for a missing relative. General Davis amused himself at their expense a short time, and sent them, the one to his quarters and the other to his home.

A few days after going into camp here, Lieut. Colonel C. H. Frederick returned to the regiment for the purpose of settling up his affairs and to bid the command "good bye." While at Nashville, he resigned his commission and was now a private citizen. His departure was witnessed with regret by the whole command. He had ever been a good, faithful officer, and a kind, good friend to the men of the regiment.

Major J. C. Winters, having returned from his leave of absence, now assumed command of the regiment, nd Captain Paine, that of Major. Captain Stookey again taking command of his company. After the capture of Adjutant Phillips, Lieutenant Minnett, of company D, was appointed Adjutant.

While the regiment lay at Murfreesboro', the following young men were deservedly promoted to the rank of First Lieutenant: Reuben Maddox, company F, I. M. Vanosdel, company K, Charles Doolittle, company I, A. Sanderson, company B, S. Eleric, company A, and Hiram Wendt, company G.

To that of Second Lieutenant: —— Curtis, company C, H. C. Baughman, company F, D. L. Korhamer, company I, Fred. N. Boyer, company H, —— Irwin, company D, and —— Anderson, company B.

To that of Captain: Hamilton W. Hall, company F, Adjutant Minnett, company D, Henry Wiley, company H, S. L. Burris, company G, I. Henderson, company C, D. Bagley, company A, Samuel West, company I.

These young men, with one or two exceptions, were enlisted as privates in the ranks. They have all been faithful soldiers, doing their duty manfully, both in time of battle and in camp. At Pea Ridge, at Perryville and Stone River they were among the bravest of the brave.

After laying in camp a few days, the regiment again moved out towards Franklin, but not so far as before. The enemy was now threatening another point in our lines, between Murfreesboro' and Franklin, and to strengthen this point General Davis moved out with his Division. No serious attack was made, and the regiment returned to camp. The lines were now shortened, and the camp all moved up nearer town. As soon as the camps were arranged, the regiments were set to work building fortifications. Until the 24th of June, work at the fortifications and picket duty was all that was required of the Fifty-Ninth. In building forts, and digging entrenchments, one-third or one-half the regiment was employed at a time. In doing picket duty, the whole regiment moved out to the lines, and remained there from five to ten days at a time.

One day, while on picket, Walter C. Wyker, of Company K, was standing guard at his post, near the pike bridge across Stone River, some rebel cavalry came in sight, a mile or two down the pike, and, to get a better view of them, Wyker stepped upon a large rock near by, and, in bringing his gun up after him, struck the lock against the rock, and fired it off, the load lodging in his bowels, killing him in a few seconds. He was brought to camp, and buried with the honors of war. He was a faithful soldier, and an agreeable mess-mate, and was universally respected by the members of his company.

Here, for the first time since leaving Boonville, Missouri, the regiment had the privilege of attending church regularly every Sabbath, and frequently during the week.

The writer's diary of the 17th of May, has the following:

"I have just returned from hearing an excellent sermon, spoken by the Reverend Colonel Granville Moody. Colonel Moody was my favorite preacher, of the Methodist Church in Oxford, Ohio, more than twenty-five years ago. I have never seen him, from that day till this. It may well be believed that his appearance brought to mind many pleasant thoughts of old times. I was again sitting in the old familiar seat, in the old brick church, of my boyhood days. Although the preacher's head has now become silvered o'er with age, his voice and looks are but little changed. His sermon was to me a 'feast of reason and a flow of soul.' His text was: 'Choose ye this day whom ye will serve. If the Lord is God, serve him.' His remarks were listened to with the most wrapped attention, and, I think, made quite an impression on the soldiers. I would that there were more such preachers in the army. Colonel Moody commands an Ohio regiment, and is a fighting Colonel. His regiment was in the thickest of the fight at Stone River, and did good execution. While he was speaking, I could not help but think of the vast amount of good he has been the instrument, in the hands of God, in doing in the world. For thirty years his words of entreaty have been spoken to thousands of anxious hearers, every Sabbath, to turn from the evil of their ways, and seek the paths of righteousness and peace. Can he be otherwise than happy?—happy in the consciousness of having done his duty towards God and man. His sermon was preached in one of the block houses inside a fort. It was a novel sight to see the preparations for dealing death and destruction to our fellow beings, surrounding the minister of peace on earth and good will to men.

"When I came back to camp I found that an order had been issued to turn over to the Quartermaster all extra baggage belonging to the men—such as blankets, clothing, etc.,—leaving them only one blanket each, one suit of clothes, an extra pair of drawers, an extra pair of socks, and an extra shirt. This looks towards an early move of some kind—an advance, perhaps, towards the enemy."

Lieutenant J. H. Knight is now Acting Quartermaster of the regiment, Lieutenant Brasher not having, as yet, returned from his parole.

David Thompson, of Company K, returned to the regiment, from Nashville, on the 16th of April. He was reported to the Surgeon the next morning at sick call. On the following day he was sent to the general field hospital, with well-developed symptoms of small-pox, and on the 21st he expired.

James Slusser, of Company F, was brought to the hospital, with dysentery, about the middle of June. He soon became convalescent, with a very good prospect of soon returning to his company in good health; but, when the regiment marched, on the 24th, he was yet unfit for duty, and was, consequently, left at the general field hospital. A relapse soon followed, and he, also, died.

In the latter part of April, one Doctor Kelly reported himself to Major Winters, with a commission as First Surgeon of the Fifty-Ninth Illinois Regiment. He was an entire stranger to all concerned, but his commission gave him authority to remain and take charge of the sick men of the regiment. He soon proved himself qualified for the position, and the boys were well pleased with the imposition.

CHAPTER XXVII.

On the 15th of June the regiment went out on picket to remain ten days. Their picket post was on the Shelbyville Pike, about two miles south of Stone River.

On the 23d of June orders were received at camp to strike tents, and move out with the train on the 24th. Consequently, on the morning of the 24th, the train moved down the pike to where the regiment had been standing picket. The regiment was already gone, and the train followed after, taking the direction of Liberty Gap. The day was very disagreeable; a drizzling rain had set in early in the morning and continued all day, wetting everything and everybody completely. In this plight the men lay on their arms all night. They were now in the neighborhood of the Gap, and it was reported that the enemy had a strong force there.

The morning of the 25th was dark and cloudy, but the troops were early astir, and soon on the advance towards the Gap. About noon the enemy were observed in force immediately in front. A disposition was speedily made of our forces, and the Fifty-Ninth was sent out as flankers, or rather as advanced skirmishers, on the right flank of the Division. Fortunately for the Fifty-Ninth, this move kept them from entering the engagement, only as skirmishers, as the fighting was all done in another part of the field. The regiment, however, skirmished pretty lively with the

CAPT. HENRY WILEY.

CAPT. J. JOHNSON.

LIEUT. H.C. BAUGHMAN.

LIEUT. D.L. KORHAMMER.

LIEUT. FRED. N. BOYER.

LIEUT. J. VANOSDELL.

LIEUT. HIRAM WENT.

LIEUT. JOS. ELERIC.

enemy all the afternoon. Some of the rebels were hit by our balls, as the boys could see them fall, or crawl from their hiding places badly wounded. The trees behind which the boys concealed themselves were frequently hit by the balls from the rebel guns, but none of the regiment was injured. On other parts of the Pass there was heavy fighting until evening, when the enemy fell back and gave our men possession.

The command held the ground until about three in the morning, when it was silently withdrawn and marched on towards Tullahoma. It was said that the enemy withdrew about the same time, neither army having any desire to renew the contest.

The march now continued daily until the 3d day of July, when the Division again went into camp at Winchester, Tennessee.

The march from Murfreesboro' to Winchester was very fatiguing. It rained almost incessantly, keeping the men continually wet, and making the roads very muddy and the streams high. The rebels, on their retreat, destroyed the bridge across Elk River, and in consequence our army was compelled to wade it. At the point where the Fifty-Ninth crossed, the water was waist deep to the men and the current very swift. Two or three of the boys would lock arms, and by assisting each other would succeed in forcing their way over. Several who braved the flood single-handed were swept away and carried a considerable distance down stream before they could effect a landing. The enemy continued to retreat from Liberty Gap, through Tullahoma, Manchester, Winchester, and Stevenson, Alabama, towards Chattanooga; so that our infantry did not overtake them before going into camp at Winchester.

The brigade of Colonel Post went into camp one

(14)

mile east of the town, and in advance of any troops belonging to the corps. The Fifty-Ninth, as usual, being the picket regiment. This was pleasing to the boys, as it gave them the privilege of the country, and an easy access to blackberries, peaches, potatoes, etc. The camp is pleasantly situated, and if the weather becomes fair the boys can enjoy themselves.

Soon after arriving here, Lieutenant Brasher, Quartermaster, and Captain Clayton Hale, (now Major Hale.) returned to the regiment. After the resignation of Lieutenant Colonel Frederick, Major Winters was promoted to the position of Lieutenant Colonel, and Clayton Hale to that of Major. Frank Clark, of Company A, now received the appointment of Adjutant.

The routine of camp life now commenced in earnest; policing, guard and picket duty, foraging and amusements of various kinds occupies the time of the regiment. The history of one day is the repetition of the preceding one, and so on.

Winchester is ninety-five miles south of Nashville, and is an old dilapidated place of perhaps eight hundred inhabitants, mostly secesh. The country around is very well improved and quite productive, but thinly populated at this time, as the citizens have, many of them, gone with the rebel army. There are several families remaining in town, but the men folks have disappeared, leaving only the women and children. Of the former there are quite a number, and many of them are young and good looking. These are an attraction for the young bloods of the army, and those of the Fifty-Ninth are very attentive. The tediousness of camp life is very much relieved by a few hours spent in the society of interesting young ladies now and then.

After a few days of idleness in camp, the boys get

very mischievous, and if there is any whisky to be had the monotony is broken by some serious termination to the pranks being played.

One evening, after imbibing pretty freely, the boys were about getting into a general engagement, when Sergeant ———, of company E, supposing it to be his duty to keep the peace, interfered. This proceeding was resented, and in the melee the Sergeant was severely cut with a knife, in the hands of one Davis, of another company. Davis immediately fled, and was never heard of afterwards. The Sergeant was taken to the hospital, to have his wound attended to. The wound was inflicted by a sharp instrument, and penetrated through the muscles of the back, into the lower lobe of the right lung. The cut on the surface was about four inches in length, and on the surface of the lung half an inch in length, deep enough to afford a full breathing surface. At every motion of the lungs the air rushed in and out of this opening as through the mouth of a bellows. When brought to the tent, the man was in a dying condition. His life was rapidly going out at the opening in the lung. The old Hospital Steward was in favor of immediately closing the wound by sewing the lips together, but the two young Assistant Surgeons, Doctors Bunce and Gaston, (Gaston had a few days before been commissioned from the ranks of the One Hundred-and-Second Illinois Regiment, to the position of Second Assistant Surgeon of the Fifty-Ninth,) overruled the idea, under the impression that by closing the wound the blood would have no egress, and by its accumulation inwardly, cause injury to the patient. The man was dying, as every one could see. His pulse was failing rapidly, and a few hours would undoubtedly finish his career. Doctor Kelly, who was in town, was sent for—came, and for appearance sake, as he said, put a couple of stitches in the wound. By this time the pulse had entirely disappeared from the wrist, and the Doctors left the tent, not doubting but that the man would soon be dead. As soon as the Surgeons left, the Steward carefully closed the wound with a compress, and caused the man to lay on that side so as to keep the compress to its place. As soon as this was done the breathing passed through the natural channel—the mouth—and in an hour the pulse could be distinctly felt at the wrist, and in the morning the Doctors were surprised to find the Sergeant, not only still living, but bright and cheerful. In ten days the man was well. Ignorance is bliss, but not always safe for the patient.

Doctor Kelly here resigned his commission as Surgeon, and Doctor Bunce immediately applied for and received a commission in his stead.

Indications now point strongly towards another move. A general inspection of the troops and trains almost always precedes a forward movement of the army, and this is now going on in this department. The next move will be across the Cumberland Mountains, and the trains must all be in good condition, or they will never stand the trip. It is only about three miles to the foot of these mountains in a direct course from here, but it is said that we must pass through Cowen before we can climb them, which is ten or twelve miles away. Cowen is a station on the Nashville and Chattanooga Railroad, and is near the entrance of the tunnel which here runs through the mountain.

On the 17th of August, the army evacuated Winchester, and camped at the foot of the mountain, to be in readiness for crossing on the following morning. The

18th was spent in getting the artillery and trains to the top of the mountain—the regiments having to assist in dragging the heavy cannon and heavy loaded wagons over the most difficult places. The 19th completed the crossing, and the troops bivouaced at the eastern foot of the mountain until morning. The march was continued on the 20th, until a convenient camp was reached near Stevenson, Alabama.

Stevenson is a small town at the junction of the Nashville and Chattanooga Railroad with the Memphis and Charleston Railroad. It is twenty-five miles from Chattanooga, and three miles from the Tennessee River. It is one hundred and twenty miles by rail from Nashville. The camp of the Fifty-Ninth is one mile from town, near the right bank of the famous Battle Creek, and within about the same distance of a high conical-shaped mountain, at the foot of which nestles the little town of Stevenson.

On the 28th the First and Second Brigades of Davis' Division moved out, and the probability was that the Third would soon follow. This the men were willing for, as they usually enjoy the march, in pleasant weather, better than much laying in camp. After a few days in camp the routine of camp life becomes tiresome, and the men wish for a change. Sickness usually increases in proportion to the length of time spent in lying idle in camp, showing that it is more agreeable to be moving occasionally. In camp there are many more indulgences in the way of gormandizing, to be sure, than on the march; but the mind, also, has its influence in preserving the health of the soldier. On the march the mind is withdrawn from brooding over the sacrifices made, and a longing for the return of those home comforts and associations which have been so long left behind. The anticipations of coming events, the changes of scenery, both of a natural and artificial character, such as hills and dales, valleys and mountains, rivers and creeks, springs and rivulets, large plantations, with their fine mansions and negro cabins, beautiful groves and lawns, or the isolated log hut of the native forester—all tending to relieve the mind of "brooding melancholy," preserve the health, and restore the convalescent, by their ever-changing attractions to the soldier, as he passes them on the march.

The sick were now sent to the general field hospital, at Stevenson, and, on the morning of the 30th, the regiment struck tents, and moved out. Passing through Stevenson, it proceeded, by a short and direct road, to the Tennessee River. Here it bivouaced till a pontoon bridge was in readiness for crossing upon. About four o'clock in the evening the brigade crossed over, and went into camp one mile distant from the river.

The 30th of August was a beautiful day, and, while awaiting the opportunity to cross, the boys amused themselves bathing in the river. The river here was three-quarters of a mile wide, and many of the men swam from one shore to the other, apparently without much difficulty. It was very amusing to stand on the bank and witness the feats of agility performed by these aquatic actors. After witnessing this lively scene, the writer and Lieutenant Sanderson, of Company A, seated themselves in the shade, near the pontoons, to witness the activity of the scene in that vicinity. Just below the bridge was the only place where the mules could be taken to water, and here the hundreds of mules and horses belonging to the trains were now being brought. Each driver brought six mules, fastened together, so that, by riding one, the others could be led without difficulty. On coming to the water there was such a crowd of them that a great deal of trouble was sometimes required to get them out without becoming considerably entangled. Swearing is a universal practice amongst M. D.'s, and now it was remarkable. It seemed as though each one tried to do more of it than any one else could. The writer had noticed that not one had left the water without leaving many curses resting on the "souls" of his poor mules. He finally remarked to the Lieutenant that he believed all mule-drivers, without an exception, would swear.

"It seems so," said the Lieutenant, "but yonder is a fellow who has been trying to disentangle his mules for some time, and he has not yet used an oath."

Patiently the fellow worked for sometime longer, but to no purpose. The mules were very stubborn, and resisted all entreaty to come to shore in order. Patience now ceases to be a virtue, and he let out—and, of all the swearing that had been heard that day, his was most satanic—'twas awful. The Lieutenant gave it up, and acknowledged that all M. D.'s would swear.

Colonel Post's brigade was now constituted rear guard to the corps train, and was, of course, the last to cross the river, and will be the last to cross the Sand Mountain, which now looms up before us. The crossing will be most difficult. The road is said to be very rugged, and in many places so steep that it will be impossible for the teams to pull the wagons up. The passage of the Alps, in miniature, is before us, and Colonel Post, in size and stature, as he directs the men in their labors, brings to mind the "Little Corporal," as he is represented in the "passage of those alpine hights."

Early in the morning the ascent of the train commences. The four regiments of the brigade have gone on, and been distributed along the ascent by detachments, so as to be in readiness to assist any of the teams that should be unable to make the "riffle." The road, in its tortuous course, was frequently obstructed by huge flat rock, broken square, so that the wagon-wheels would have to be lifted twelve or fifteen inches perpendicularly to get over them. At such places, as many men as could get near the wagon would lay hold and hoist it, and then the mules could again proceed. About two o'clock the trains succeeded in reaching the top of the mountain, and the brigade then moved on for two or three miles, and took up quarters for the night. The descent was almost as difficult as the ascent, and the brigade was again stationed at the difficult places, as before. Where the declivity was steep large ropes were fastened to the rear of the wagons, and grasped by as many soldiers as was necessary to keep the wagon from rushing upon and crushing the mules in front. The crossing of Sand Mountain was accomplished, and the brigade again went into quarters.

From the 2d day of September until the 6th, the trains were moved by easy stages towards the foot of Lookout Mountain, at a point called Valley Head. Here they went into corral to await the movements of the army in the front. The brigade, of course, also went into quarters. Valley Head is about forty miles from Chattanooga, and about the same distance from Rome, Ga. It is enclosed by Sand Mountain on the west, and Lookout Mountain on the east. It extends between these mountains from this point up to the Tennessee River. It is a very narrow valley, and is poorly improved. An occasional plantation only being met with. Here, at Valley Head, are two or three good plantations, but very much impaired by the depredations of the soldier, both rebel and Union. Here the fences had been burned from many of the fields, and some buildings destroyed by the rebels before the Union soldiers came to the neighborhood. The plantation on which the brigade was now camped, was in a measure destroyed by the rebel soldiers. Major Winston, the owner of the plantation, had been opposed to the war, and had suffered these depredations in consequence.

On the 10th, the trains were again in motion. They moved to the foot of the mountain, and again went into corral. The Fifty-Ninth Regiment moved to the top of the mountain, and bivouaced about two miles in advance of the wagons. Here it lay until the 13th, when it was again moved down to the foot of the mountain.

The road up the Lookout Mountain is here very good, and offers no great obstructions to the passage of the trains. It winds around all the steep acclivities, and misses all the large rock that project from the sides of this mountain. Huge masses of rock are everywhere hanging from the top and sides of this mountain; in some places affording "look out" points, from which may be seen the valley beneath, and the mountains around as far as vision can extend. It is from these points that the mountain derives its name of "Lookout." A few rods from the road is one of these projections, allowing a full view of Valley Head with all its surroundings.

On the 18th, the brigade again ascended the mountain, and made a forced march of about twenty-five miles towards Chattanooga, going into camp sometime after night, not far below Dug Gap, and near the eastern summit of the mountain.

The 19th was spent in camp, with orders to be ready to move at a moment's warning. A battle was now momentarily expected to take place in the valley below, and the boys were very restless. Not far from camp was a famous "look out," and hundreds of the soldiers visited it through the day for the purpose of viewing the "landscape o'er." From this point, the whole of Lookout, or Chattanooga Valley could be seen. For miles the valley is spread out to the view in all its variagated loveliness. Plantations, with their white mansions visible, here and there are seen, nestled as it were, in dark, deep forests; wreaths of smoke ascending from the depths of other clumps of dark, dense foliage, indicates the habitations of other dwellers in the valley, yet no house is seen. Nearer by, the open fields, with their herds of cattle and their flocks in pasture, as yet undisturbed by the ruthless soldier, and close by the planter's house and negro cabins. These may be seen with the naked eye. With a field glass or telescope, another feature is added to the scene. Soldiers, both cavalry and infantry could be seen marching in the distance, far over towards the Chicamauga. From this deep valley, now comes up the booming of distant cannon, adding deep interest to the scene. The armies are as yet only feeling for each others weakness—to-morrow they will try each others strength.

All day the point was crowded with eager eyes, looking over that vast field of vision. And in the morning, as early as the light permitted, some returned to see what change the night might have produced, and they were well satisfied with their early visit. Before the sun began to shed his rays above the horizon, the scene presented in the valley below reminded one of an ocean of water. The smoke and fog had settled through the night on all the lower lands of the valley, and resembled in appearance the blue of the deep waters of the ocean. The ridges in the valley elevated the tops of the trees growing upon them, above this canopy of smoke, and gave them the appearance of islands in the ocean. As soon as the god of day began to pencil the horizon with his rays, the oceanic illusion vanished. At first a faint tinge of red appeared, and from this the redness gradually increased and grew broader and deeper until his whole broad face was visible. Redder and more fiery than any living coal was his appearance. It was not the white heat of noon-day, but the most brilliant red immaginable. The sight was most magnificent—most sublime. The setting sun, as witnessed from the "point" on the opposite side of the mountain was most beautiful—but this was most sublime.

At seven o'clock the order came to march. At eight the brigade was in motion, and in an hour it was wending its way across the valley towards the battlefield of Chickamauga. About twelve o'clock it had reached the "Crawfish Springs," and formed in position to resist an expected attack from the enemy. Before getting to the Springs rebels had been seen hovering on the flank of our command, and one or two shots had been fired at our advanced skirmishers.

On arriving at the Springs it was ascertained that the enemy had intercepted our march with too heavy a force for our brigade to advance against, and that he was also throwing a large force upon our right and rear. This was more than had been anticipated, and it became evident that there was now only one course to pursue, and that was to get away from the Springs in the best way possible. The only way to do this was to take the road towards Chattanooga immediately—

this was done. The train moved on in advance, and the regiments followed. The command bivouaced about five miles from Chattanooga, and lay on their arms that night. The next day it moved two miles farther towards town, and on the morning of the 22d continued the retreat until it reached the lines at Chattanooga. When within about one mile of the lines the enemy began to throw shells into the ranks. The battery nearest the command from the lines in town, being apprised of the approach of the rebels, now came out and replied so vigorously to the rebel battery that it soon withdrew and the brigade marched in unhurt. In coming from the mountain to the Springs several stragglers were taken prisoners by the rebels. The Fifty-Ninth lost three or four men in this way. Had the brigade been one hour later in coming up to Chattanooga it would have been cut off and captured. The army had all fallen back the day before, and Post's command was the only one outside of the strong position in front of town. The position was now so well chosen, and our lines so compact, that the enemy dare not attack it.

The campaign for the summer was now over, and the army intrenched itself at Chattanooga. Works were immediately constructed sufficient in strength and magnitude, to resist any attempt on the part of the enemy to take the town, and the army quietly awaited further developments. The campaign had been a severe and tedious one. The men were worn out and needed rest. Their clothing was becoming thin and the weather disagreeable, so that they began to suffer for the want of comfortable covering to protect them from the storm and against the cold and chilly nights. It was fully time they were also better supplied with food as well as clothing. Rations were becoming very short. One half rations of bread and one quarter rations of bacon was all the most of the men could get, and some of them, for a time, did not get even so much as that. For about ten days after the occupation of Chattanooga the men of the Fifty-Ninth Illinois Regiment received five crackers each for three days' rations, with about the same proportion of bacon. This was a near approach to starvation.

The enemy now invested Chattanooga closely; artillery firing was practiced daily, and many a laugh was had at the expense of the rebel shells. Thousands of shells were thrown at Chattanooga during the seige, without doing any damage of any kind, except, perhaps, in one case. It was said that a negro man, while bringing water from the spring, was shot through by a solid six-pound ball. This, however, is doubted.

One of the boys of Company K, of the Fifty-Ninth, was frying his ration of bacon one morning when a twelve pounder struck his pan and knocked it into the "middle of next week," and the boy lost his bacon.

The Fifty-Ninth lay behind breast-works on the left bank of Chattanooga Creek, and the rebel pickets were stationed on the opposite bank, not over two hundred yards distant. The water from the creek supplied both parties, and meetings would frequently take place between the boys and the rebels, when they would have a friendly chat and a tobacco or newspaper trade. An understanding was had between the parties that there should be no shooting at each other. These friendly relations continued until the regiment was removed to another part of the field.

The month of October was a very wet, rainy month, and caused some sickness in the regiment. Several of the men were compelled to give up doing duty and go to hospital, amongst whom was Sergeant William Curtis, of Company K, David M. Minard, of Company A, Sergeant Marcus D. Leigh, of Company F, and John B. Forester, of Company F. These were all young men of exemplary reputations for good moral conduct and soldierly behavior in all their intercourse with the regiment. They had undergone all the hardships, and endured all the exposure and fatigue of all the marches and campaigns, and been in all the battles the regiment had experienced since being in the service. The friends and relations of these young men have now to mourn them as numbered among the honored dead. Sergeant Curtis died at Chattanooga on the 26th of October, 1863, William M. Minard on the 2d of December, 1863, Sergeant Leigh died at Nashville on the 26th of December, 1863, soon after being removed from Chattanooga, and John B. Forester on the 7th day of January, 1864, at Louisville, Kentucky.

About the middle of October the regiment crossed the Tennessee River, and went up into the Sequatchie Valley, with a train, after forage. It was gone three days, and had a good time of it. In the Valley the boys found plenty of hogs, chickens, honey, and other luxuries, which were unsparingly appropriated. An order to go foraging was always hailed with delight, as it promised better living than was usually to be had in camp.

The question is frequently discussed in camp, "Why re we not better provided for—why are we compelled to live on hard bread and old bacon?" We are fighting our own battles, at our own expense, and we are able and willing to pay for good living. Why do we not get it? Is the question an unreasonable one? Can any one satisfactorily explain the reason why our soldiers are restricted to a certain kind of food? and such food, too, as no man thinks of living on at home. The expense of providing good palatable diet—such as bread, with salt and shortening in it, instead of that which is so hard and tasteless—with potatoes, beans, fruit, etc., etc.,—would be more than saved by preserving the health of the men, and thereby keeping them on duty, instead of having them become scorbutic and worthless to the Government, and not only worthless, but a useless expense. After the scurvy is established in the system of the soldier, a more generous diet is resorted to for the removal of the disease. Why not provide the diet as a preventive to the disease?

CHAPTER XXVIII.

On the 25th of October, the brigade left Chattanooga for Shell Mound. Early in the morning, before the sun had risen, the Fifty-Ninth broke camp and marched down to the river. The other regiments of the brigade were crossing over on the pontoon bridge below town, and the Fifty-Ninth fell into column at the proper time and crossed over.

The bridge at this point is about three hundred yards long, and requires fifty-two pontoons to float it. A few nights before the regiment crossed, the rebels sent a large raft, made of heavy timber, down the river, which striking the bridge, stove it into pieces. It did not take long to repair it, and very little damage was done by this sharp trick.

After crossing, the command took the road leading down through the river bottom lands for five miles, when it reached the foot of the Sequatchie Mountain. Here it rested a short time, and the men refreshed themselves with a hard tack and a slice of bacon. Before them now looms up a mountain, around the side of which winds a road four miles long, which they must climb. The bugle sounds, and the march up the mountain commences. Had there been nothing to attract attention on the way, the march would have been a toilsome one, but as it was, the men did not think of getting weary. The road in many places was marked by objects of much interest on the side of the road next the mountain. Masses of rock of all shapes and of every dimension meet the view. Some of these appeared just ready to fall, and crush the column as it passed. Here was one forming a perpendicular wall, of a hundred feet in hight, and three hundred in length; and then another of as large dimensions, in appearance like to an old ancient castle set in the side of the mountain. Here is another, with an opening to a cave within, of unknown extent. There issues a stream of limpid water large enough to turn the wheels of fortune; and not far from this, a beautiful jet of pure, cold water bursts, as it were, from out the solid rock, and trickles along, way down the mountain, in pearly drops. At the foot of the mountain, the Tennessee River urges its way through its narrow rock-bound channel, in billowy grandeur. It is only now and then that its waters can be seen from the line of march, but when they are, it is only to cause a frequent turning of the eye in that direction to get another glimpse.

In this passage up the mountain, there is one place, of half a mile in length, which is called the "Narrows." From the high bluffs, on the opposite side of the river, a minnie ball may be thrown against the rocks above the road, on the Sequatchie Mountain. Several mules and one or two men had been killed while passing these narrows by rebel sharp shooters, from the bluffs across the river. Two or three shots were fired at the column now passing, but no one was hit. About one o'clock the regiment arrived at the summit of the mountain, and there halted for dinner.

After dinner and an hour's rest, the march was continued. The road now taken is called the Old Ridge

(15)

Road. It leads along the summit of this ridge for twenty miles. Sometimes the ridge is just broad enough for the passage of a single wagon, and at these places you can look down, down, down, until your head swims. There are some very good "look out" points on this ridge.

The regiment went into camp on the evening of the 26th, near one of these points, and had the pleasure of witnessing the departure of Old Sol, as he disappeared below the horizon. It was a pretty sight. During the twilight they had an opportunity of looking up and down the Sequatchie Valley, as it lay in the depths below. It had the appearance of being a very rich and finely cultivated country. Farms and farm houses were quite numerous and seemed snug and inviting.

The descent from this mountain summit commenced early on the morning of the 27th, and after ascending and descending innumerable acclivities and declivities, the regiment went into camp on the bank of the Tennessee River. Here it was expected that the command would be ferried across the river, at what was called Brown's Ferry, but after about two hours in quarters, the order came to march. It was still about seven miles to Shell Mound, and this was the distance now to be marched. The sun was setting, as the regiment moved out, and about nine o'clock it crossed the river at Shell Mound, and went into camp again.

Shell Mound is seven miles above Bridgeport, and twenty-one below Chattanooga. To get from Chattanooga here, the command had marched sixty-miles. Shell Mound derives its name from the innumerable quantity of shells that is piled up there. The entire mound is composed of muscle shell, as though they had been hauled there and tilted from the cart. Their number is most astonishing. It might be supposed that all the muscles from the first creation to the present time had made this their charnel house.

If some shrewd Yankee should ever take it into his head to load a few flat-boats with these shells, and have them pulverized and barreled up, he could make a fortune by selling the powder as a fertilizer for Northern farms. This bed of shells is ten feet deep at the river brink, and covers several acres, in some places to a greater depth.

At this place is another great curiosity—the "Negro Jack Cave," as it is called by the natives. The entrance to this cave is large—perhaps twenty feet wide, and fifteen feet to the arch above. The arch is most beautifully turned, smooth and regular. The smoke from the fires which have been kindled under this arch has given it a cloudy appearance, which is very pretty. This is a saltpetre cave, and the rebels have had very extensive works through it. Around the entrance, on the outside, are furnaces and kettles; on the inside are hundreds of filterers, or hoppers, for filtering the clay, which holds the saltpetre. On penetrating fifty or sixty feet within, the light disappears, and it is necessary to use torches or candles to see the way over the slimy hillocks of mud and broken stone, which fill the passages. The cave is said to be fifteen miles in length. There is a large stream of water running through it, which has been ascended by canoes for ten miles, from the entrance. This stream flows out from an opening a short distance to the right of the mouth of the cave, in size sufficient to turn a large grist mill. It is crossed on a plank bridge, about five hundred feet from the mouth of the cave. The water can not be seen, but a stone dropped from the bridge can be heard as it plunges into the water far below. The walls, in some places, are very rough, and in others quite smooth.

Some distance, after crossing the river, you come to a small chamber, which is very pretty. It is, perhaps, twenty feet square. The ceiling is ornamented with stalactites, resembling icicles, and the walls are perpendicular and smooth. The corners and the edges of the ceiling are as though they had been ornamented by some master workman. There are many different passages leading from the main entrance, and great attention is required, or you lose your way.

When Buell's army was here some of his boys got lost in this cave, and were three days in finding the way out, and would not then if a band of music had not went in, and blowed their instruments, which were heard by the wanderers, and thus discovered to them the direction they ought to take. While seeking their way out, these boys came across the body of a Lieutenant, who had lost his way, and thus perished. This cave received the name of "Negro Jack" because of its having been the hiding place of an old negro by that name, in an early day.

There had been a small town at Shell Mound, and the railroad depot was yet standing when our boys got there, but the next morning it was torn down to make shelters and fires for the men. It was a nice brick depot, and its destruction ought not to have been allowed. It was the last of Shell Mound City. The saltpetre works are all destroyed, and there is nothing here now of interest but the pontoon bridge across the river.

The regiments lay at Shell Mound two days, and then moved up to Whitesides, seven miles nearer Chattanooga. Here the brigade went into winter quarters.

Whiteside Station is fourteen miles below Chattanooga, and is at the foot of Raccoon Mountain, in Marion County, Tennessee. Camp is situated on the side of the mountain, just above the railroad, and is within protecting distance of the "Falling Waters" railroad bridge, now in course of reconstruction. This bridge was destroyed by the rebels on the approach of Buell's army. It was a fine structure, and cost ninety-five thousand dollars. It was five hundred feet in length, and ninety-five feet in hight.

The mountain summit is at least a thousand feet above camp. Near the top is a large ledge of rock, and just below this ledge is an opening to a coal mine. These mountains are full of coal, and there are several mines within a short distance of camp.

The chute from the one above the depot, deposits the coal near where it is loaded upon the cars for shipment. These chutes are square tunnels, made of boards. By putting the coal in at the top, it is conducted, with the rapidity of a cannon ball, to the bottom. The boys are now amusing themselves by throwing large stones into this chute, and watching them come out at the bottom. Below camp runs a small mountain stream called the "Falling Waters." On the opposite side of this stream rises another mountain, to the hight of two thousand feet. The Ninth Indiana Regiment is stationed on the summit of this mountain.

While at Chattanooga, the army was reorganized, and, instead of four regiments, there were now eight in a brigade. Colonel Post was now acting as President of a Board of Claims, and Colonel Gross, of the Thirty-Sixth Indiana, was in command of the brigade. The brigade consisted of the Fifty-Ninth Illinois, Seventy-Fifth Illinois, Eightieth Illinois, Ninth Indiana,

Thirty-Sixth Indiana, Ninety-Sixth Ohio, and Eighty-Fourth Illinois Regiments. The eighth regiment had not yet joined the brigade.

Colonel P. Sidney Post, on relinquishing the command of the First Brigade of General Davis' old division, which was consolidated in the new organization, issued the following order:

"HEADQU'RS 1ST BRIG., 1ST DIV., 20TH ARMY CORPS,
"Chattanooga, Oct. 16, '63.

"*General Order No. 51.*—In the organization of the army, this brigade will lose its indentity, and be transferred to another division and corps. Organized on the banks of the Ohio more than a year ago, it has traversed Kentucky and Tennessee, scaled the mountains of Northern Alabama and Georgia, and now terminates its existence on the south bank of the Tennessee. The year during which it has remained intact will ever be remembered as that in which the gallant armies of the West rolled back the advancing hosts of the rebellion, and extinguished the Confederacy in the valley of the Mississippi. In accomplishing this glorious achievement, you—soldiers of the First Brigade—have performed no mean part. On the laborious march you have been patient and energetic, and in the skirmish and battle second to none in stubborn valor and success. In one year you lost upon the battle-field eight hundred and fifty heroic comrades. Baptised in blood at Perryville, this brigade led the army in pursuit of the retreating foe, and again attacks him at Lancaster, whence he fled from Kentucky. In the midwinter campaign it opened the battle at Stone River, by attacking and driving the enemy from Nolensville, on the memorable 31st of December, together with the rest of the Twentieth Army Corps valiantly met the attack of the concentrated opposing army. At Liberty Gap, and in the late battle of Chickamauga, it performed well the part assigned it, and finishes its honorable career weaker in number but strong in the confidence and discipline of invincible veterans. For the able and hearty co-operations its commander has received from the officers, and for the cheerful support yielded by its gallant men, he returns his sincere thanks. No petty jealousies, no intrigue or demoralizing influences, have ever disgraced and paralized our efforts for the country's cause; and the commander unites in the just pride which all feel in the history of, and in their connection with, the First Brigade, First Division, Twentieth Army Corps.

"P. SIDNEY POST,
"Colonel Commanding Brigade.

CHAPTER XXIX.

On the morning of the 23d of November, the brigade broke up camp at Whitesides and took up the line of march towards Chattanooga. About six o'clock that evening it went into quarters at the foot of Lookout Mountain. The anticipation was that the command would cross the river the next morning and join General Sherman, who was about engaging the enemy above Chattanooga. This anticipation was not realized. Early on the morning of the 24th the men were under arms and facing the Lookout. Soon the column commenced moving, and now the object of the move became apparent—which was no less than the storming of Lookout Mountain. Is it possible that these men are to march up that rugged mountain side in the face of a relentless foe above, who are prepared to hurl destruction down upon them from the hight. Nothing daunted by the formidable task assigned them, the troops moved boldly forward. The enemy resisted stubbornly, but could not withstand the onward move of our brave men. The fight was terrific for about five hours. The Third brigade acted nobly, and the Fifty-Ninth Illinois added new laurels to her war-worn banner. Not a man wavered, but each vied with the other in urging on the advance.

Those who witnessed the maneuvering of the men—and every move could be seen from Chattanooga and the adjacent hills—expressed the greatest admiration at the masterly manner in which the regiments made their charges. The Fifty-Ninth retained an unbroken line during the whole of this arduous contest. General Hooker, who witnessed the whole affair, remarked that he never saw a more perfect line of battle maintained by any regiment, during successive charges, than was here maintained by the Fifty-Ninth Illinois. The regiment lost but one killed and three wounded. The rebels invariably over-shot us. James Medford, of Company G, was killed while in the act of shooting at the enemy.

The morning of the 25th revealed to all in the valley below the glorious flag of the Union floating over the point of Lookout.

Early on the morning of the 25th our brigade again advanced and skirmished with the enemy all the way across Chattanooga Valley to Missionary Ridge. Here the enemy attempted to make another stand. With a shout our men charged upon them with fixed bayonets and again put them to flight. In this charge the Fifty-Ninth was in the advance, and was the first regiment to reach the summit of the Ridge. Although the charge was a most dangerous one, only one man of the regiment was wounded.

The regiment lay on the Ridge that night, and at sunrise continued the pursuit. On the morning of the 28th, the command reached Ringgold, eighteen miles from Chattanooga. At this place the rebels made another stand, and the battle raged most furiously all the forenoon, but terminated in the complete rout of the enemy. The Fifty-Ninth was on the field and in line of battle, but did not become engaged.

After the battle, the Third Brigade was ordered to move five miles down the railroad towards Tunnel Hill, and ascertain how far the rebs had gone. About four miles from town a line of battle was discovered in our front, and the brigade was halted. Here it remained 'till after dark, when many fires were kindled as if it was intended to remain all night, but the men silently withdrew behind the lights and returned to town.

On the afternoon of the 30th, the brigade started on its return to Whitesides. The division returned through the Chickamauga battle field, and spent all the 1st day of December in burying the dead that had been left unburied by the rebs. After over two months' exposure, there was nothing left of the bodies but bones to bury. Hundreds of these were found and covered. They had buried their own dead, but the Union soldier was left to moulder where he fell. On the 6th day of December the regiment again went into winter quarters, in their old camp at Whitesides.

There was now a fair prospect of remaining in camp for some time, and the boys went to work in earnest to prepare themselves comfortable shanties. In a few days they were all comfortably housed, and ready for all kinds of mischief.

Corporal William A. Gilbert was left in hospital at Whitesides when the regiment marched, and soon after its return he departed this life. He was buried with the honors of war, on a pleasant spot above camp, on the side of Raccoon Mountain.

The regiment, on this expedition, was commanded by Major Clayton Hale, Lieutenant Colonel Winters having resigned and gone home, a short time before the regiment moved. Captain James H. Stookey was Acting Major. These two officers, soon afterwards, received a promotion—the one, Major Hale, received a commission as Lieutenant-Colonel; the other, Captain

Stookey, a commission as Major of the Fifty-Ninth Regiment Illinois Volunteers. Captain Stookey's promotion was highly pleasing to the men of the regiment. By his unassuming manners, and kindly disposition, he had obtained the good will and esteem, not only of the men belonging to his own company, but of the whole regiment. He had proven himself a brave, good officer, and one of the best tacticians in the regiment. His promotion was richly merited. Major Hale had never taken any pains to conciliate the feelings of the men towards himself, but had ever been reticent in his manners towards the private soldier, and, consequently, had lost that feeling of regard which friendly communings, and social manners, always engenders.

CHAPTER XXX.

While the regiment lay at Ringgold, an order was received at head-quarters authorizing the enlistment of veteran volunteers, to serve for three years, or during the war, with the proviso that those who had been in service for two years would be accepted, and none others; and that each should receive a bounty of four hundred and two dollars, and a thirty days furlough; and, also, that their old term of service should expire, and their new term commence, on the day of enlistment. Some fifteen or twenty re-enlisted immediately, and, after returning to Whitesides, some two hundred and fifty others entered their names for the veteran service. This, according to an act of the War Department, constituted the Fifty-Ninth a veteran regiment. It, therefore, now lost its identity as the Fifty-Ninth Regiment Illinois Volunteers, and assumed the name of Fifty-Ninth Veteran Volunteer Infantry Regiment of Illinois. The men were mustered on the 5th day of January, 1864, as veterans, and, on the 13th of February, arrived at Springfield, Illinois, to receive their promised furloughs. On their arrival, Adjutant-General Fuller addressed to them the following beautiful expression of welcome and regard:

"I congratulate you on your soldierly appearance, and the favorable auspices under which you have returned to fill up your decimated ranks. The liberal bounties offered by the Government, and the almost universal liberal policy adopted by the several counties of the State to aid and encourage enlistments, together with the high character which your regiment has deservedly acquired, will, doubtless, attract to your ranks hundreds of our patriotic and loyal young men who have awaited the return of our veteran regiments to identify their destinies and unite their fortunes with them.

"On the 21st of September, 1861, you took the field as undisciplined recruits. You now return a regiment of veteran *volunteers*, and as such are entitled to wear the badge of honor—the mark of distinction—the evidence of recognition of your country for past meritorious service.

"So great was the rush to arms in this State, in the early stages of the rebellion, you were unable to obtain admission as the Ninth Missouri. At that time our sister State of Missouri was undergoing the throes of a revolution within her own borders, and nothing but the strong arm of military power prevented her from throwing off her allegiance to the General Government, and openly espousing the cause of her enemies. Your services, and that of other Illinois regiments, did much to rescue her from the abyss of ruin into which she was plunging.

"Though you went to the field, and have returned from it unheralded, your history is not unknown, nor have your services been unnoticed. Without disparagement to others, all of whom have done so well, I can truly say that in no Illinois regiment has the State authorities and the people of the State taken a stronger interest, or felt a greater pride, than in the Fifty-Ninth. Why should they not? The rapidity of your long marches, your patient endurance, and your daring dash in battles, have rarely, if ever, been excelled. The Polish Lancers were not more fleet, nor the French Hussars more daring, nor the English veterans more unyielding, than you. And, while you have been making the circuit of Western battle-fields, as this, the general officers under whom you have served, testify of you.

"We hear of you on the 22d of September, 1861, embarking on transports at St. Louis for Jefferson City. At Jefferson City on that day, we hear of you at Otterville, on the 1st of October; at Syracuse on the 14th; at Warsaw, on the 24th; crossing the Osage on the 25th; by forced marches, at Springfield on the 3d of November; at Syracuse again on the 17th of November; at Lamoine Bridge preparing winter quarters, December 7th; at Lamoine Bridge again on the 15th; breaking camp again and marching in mud, and rain, and snow, with scanty camp and garrison equipage and half rations, for Lebanon; leaving Lebanon on the 10th of February for Springfield, as a part of General Curtis' army, to fight the rebels under Price, at that place. You arrive on the 13th, and find the enemy fled; pursuing and fighting the rear guard, you bring him to battle and fight and whip him at Dry Springs; crossing the Arkansas line on the 19th; at Cross Hollows on the 22d; and at Pea Ridge, on the 7th and 8th of March, shoulder to shoulder, with the Twenty-Fifth, Thirty-Seventh, Davidson's Battery, and other Illinois troops, you fight and win one of the most stubborn and well-contested battles of the war.

"Without rest after this terrible struggle, and the enemy leaving their dead Generals behind, and fleeing across the Ozark Mountains, you leave Pea Ridge on the 10th, and we hear of you at Cross Timbers, April

6th; at Bull Creek, April 20th; at Sulphur Rock, May 10th; and at Cape Girardeau, almost in sight of your homes, May 20th; enroute to reinforce General Halleck's army at Pittsburg Landing, stopping at Paducah a short time, on the 24th; you hear from Governor Yates, who there addressed you cheering words upon what had transpired while you were in the "wilderness;" you proceed to Hamburg Landing, and participate in the engagement of the 30th of that month. On the 3d of June we again hear from you at Booneville, Miss., in pursuit of the enemy; at Ripley, Miss., on the 30th; at Jacinto, Miss., on the 4th of July; at Iuka, Ala., on the 15th of August; at Florence, on the 24th; at Murfreesboro', September 2d; at Nashville, September 4th; at Bowling Green, on the 17th; at Louisville, on the 26th; and entering the fight at Perrysville, on the 7th of October, with three hundred and sixty-one men, and coming out of it with less than two-thirds that number.

"The distance actually marched, from the time you left Booneville, Mo., until you bivouaced at Franklin, Tenn., was two thousand five hundred and forty-seven miles. With such a record of marches and counter marches, of skirmishes and battles, you have indeed merited the compliment paid you by one of your Generals, as the 'grey hound, or fleet-footed fighting regiment of Illinois.'

"I have no time to dwell upon the honorable and brilliant part you bore in the subsequent battles of Stone River, Chickamauga and Chattanooga. Nine hundred and fifty-seven men have entered your regiment, at and since its organization. Two hundred and sixty-seven have re-enlisted as veterans. These figures tell the tale, and are more eloquent of your praise than any words which I could utter. You will be furloughed for thirty days, and at the expiration of that time, rendezvous here for re-organization. The good people of Coles, Cumberland, Edgar, Greene, Knox, Madison, McDonough, St. Clair and Warren, who have an especial interest in your fame and welfare, will welcome you with loving words and open arms. Return then, to families and friends, and receive a soldier's welcome and your country's gratitude.

"But in your thankfulness to a kind Providence which has permitted you to return to receive your children's love, your brother's friendship, and your parent's blessings, forget not to console the bereaved. Bleeding hearts await you to learn the last tidings of those who have wasted away by disease, or been stricken down by your sides. Comfort bereaved ones by the assurance that your fallen comrades maintained the fair fame of a Union soldier while living, and died while manfully battling for their country and their country's cause.

"General White, in whom I recognize a true gentleman, a gallant officer and an old friend, and under whom you served on many long marches, and at the memorable battle of Pea Ridge, I feel assured can not resist the temptation to address his old comrades, now impatient to hear him."

General White then said: "Fellow soldiers of the Fifty-Ninth. The language usually employed at the meeting of friends, does not express the emotion experienced by me on this occasion. In you I recognize not only patriots, who have devoted themselves to the rescue of our country from the hands of traitors, but men with whom it was my fortune to share the toils, privations and dangers of the soldiers' life in camp, on the march and on the battle-field. The bond of affection thus created is well known to officers and soldiers; and may it never be broken."

After a few further remarks, the General retired and the men, on the reception of their furloughs, dispersed to their beloved homes, until duty again called them to the field.

On the departure of the "veterans" for Springfield, those who did not re-enlist, to the number of eighty, were assigned to duty with the Seventy-Fifth Illinois Regiment. Here they remained until the Fifty-Ninth returned to the field, when they rejoined it and continued in their old companies until their term of service terminated, which was on the 6th day of September, 1864, three years and one month after being mustered in at St. Louis. Their three years' service really expired on the 6th day of August, but by some chicanery or other they were compelled to serve one month beyond that time, and even then did not get their discharge papers until about the 15th of September, being kept in idleness and suspense for ten days after being relieved from duty. The last month of their service, which was the month of their conscription, was the most arduous and most dangerous of any during their three years' servitude. It was the last month of General Sherman's campaign against Atlanta. On the last day of their term of service, the 6th of September, they made one of the most desperate charges on the rebel line of works that had ever been made by any other regiment during the campaign. Several of the veterans were killed and many wounded; and one of the non-vets, Jacob Rader, of Company F, whose term of service, according to an original act of the War Department, had expired on the 24th of June, over two months previous, that being the day of his enlistment,

(16)

was severely if not mortally wounded. Another one, James Rowsey, of the same company, was mortally wounded in the head, and died in a few days afterwards. His term expired on the 6th of August, one month previous, but his life was sacrificed to the unjust conscription now being practiced upon those who could not consistently re-enlist as veterans. Whether this injustice was due to any act of the War Department, or to the neglect or inhuman feelings of the commanders in the army is left for others than the writer to decide.

One Donathy, of Company K, also a non-veteran, was killed on the 4th day of July, while making a charge on the enemy's lines. The remainder of the non-veterans finally left the army on the 12th day of September, and, after much difficulty and great risk, arrived at Louisville, Kentucky, where they were paid, and received an honorable discharge, and were now permitted to return to their homes. Long may they live to enjoy the peace and comfort they so richly deserve! May their lives be prolonged on the earth until the last enemy of the free institutions of this glorious Union be called hence, to render up the final accounts to Him who judgeth the quick and the dead.

> "Cheers, cheers, for our heroes!
> Not those who wear stars;
> Not those who wear eagles,
> And leaflets, and bars;
> We know they are gallant,
> And honor them too,
> For bravely maintaining
> The Red, White, and Blue!"
>
> "But cheers for our soldiers,
> Rough, wrinkled and brown;
> The men who make heroes,
> And ask no renown;

Unselfish, untiring,
Intrepid and true,
The bulwark surrounding
The Red, White, and Blue!"

"Our patriot soldiers!
When treason arose,
And Freedom's own children
Assailed her as foes;
When anarchy threatened
And order withdrew,
They rallied to rescue
The Red, White, and Blue!"

"Upholding our banner,
On many a field,
The doom of the traitor
They valiantly sealed;
And worn with the conflict,
Found vigor anew,
Where victory greeted
The Red, White, and Blue."

"Yet, loved ones have fallen—
And still when they sleep,
A sorrowing nation
Shall silently weep;
And Spring's fairest flowers,
In gratitude, strew,
O'er those who have cherished
The Red, White, and Blue!"

"But glory, immortal,
Is waiting them now,
And chaplets unfading
Shall bind every brow,
When called by the trumpet,
At Time's great review,
They stand, who defended
The Red, White, and Blue."

THE END.

www.ingramcontent.com/pod-product-compliance
Lightning Source LLC
Chambersburg PA
CBHW031730230426
43669CB00007B/302